Scrawls on the Walls of the Soul

Book Two in the Quantum Shaman™ Series

Della Van Hise

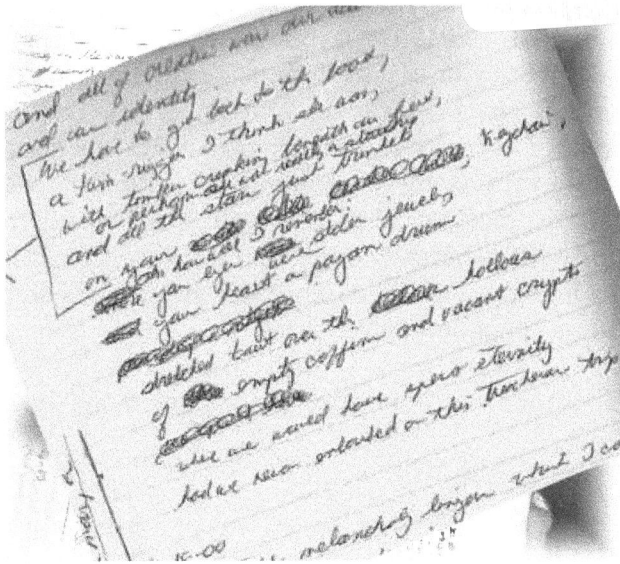

*"It's not your neatly typed essays that interest me,
but the scrawls on the walls of your soul."*
(Orlando – 2005)

Scrawls On the Walls of the Soul
by Della Van Hise

Copyright © 2012, 2013, 2018
by Della Van Hise & Quantum Shaman™

ISBN: 978-0-9896938-2-0

A Quantum Shaman™ Book
Published by Eye Scry Publications
www.eyescrypublications.com

Introduction
The Dark Enlightenment

It was sometime in May of 2000 when my higher self, who answers to the name of Orlando, essentially threw me out of the quantum cosmic classroom and said, "I've taught you everything I can. Now it's time to take that knowledge and slam it up against the walls of the real world. If it remains intact and survives the brutality to which it will be subjected, you will get a gold star next to your name and be allowed to proceed to the next level." No mention was made of what this next level might be, or if, indeed, it truly existed. As always, Orlando was cryptic, yet at the same time brutally honest.

I was elated – patted myself on the back and took a bow! I had been promoted! And yet... a moment later, I was devastated. Surely there was more to know? And how would I navigate without Orlando to guide me? Was he actually *leaving* me?

What I didn't know then, of course, was that his casual comment to the effect that he had taught me all he could was also a can of wormholes. He had taught me all he *could* because I had come to a point where I had to test my knowledge experientially before I could learn anything more.

I had been in that quantum cosmic classroom since November of 1994 – almost six years of near-total immersion in what I have come to call, simply, The Path. For those not familiar with my first book or my website, *Quantum Shaman*™, let me say that the classroom was anything *but* a classroom. There were no books, other than the ones I was required to write – mostly in the form of my journals and personal correspondences with other seekers and facilitators around the world. There were no course materials, no curriculum, nothing but the questions themselves which fueled the journey.

There were things about the "classroom" that defy conventional explanation, which are chronicled *in Quantum*

Shaman: Diary of a Nagual Woman. Mysterious letters from an unknown source. Happenings that had elements of a haunting at times, alien encounters at others, with a hint of inexplicable interdimensionality thrown in just to keep things from getting dull. Whenever I would think I had it all figured out, some other monkey wrench would inject itself into the machinery and reset the entire equation back to zero. And so The Path is also referred to as The Quantum Rabbit Hole at the Edge of the Nothing. Jump in one side, you may come out in another universe or in another time. Try to figure it out, you'll only hurt yourself.

For purposes of *this* book, all that is really necessary to know is that Orlando is my mentor, my higher self, my muse, and – some might say – my personal devil and guardian angel. This is the nature of the shaman's double – to be what we need it to be – and at the time in my life when these occurrences were at their peak, I needed Orlando to be my teacher in relation to the query: *"Is this life all there is?"* To some, that may be the wrong question. To me, it was the *only* question, burning a hole in the fabric of my entire being. I had had some encounters with my mortality, had spent a considerable amount of time sitting on the edge of the abyss as a result, and had finally reached a plateau of abject spiritual surrender – which is the *only* location in the multiverse where the student is ready and the teacher *can* appear.

If I had to wrap a timeframe around these events, or condense it all down to 100 words or less, it would be impossible – and such is the nature of metaphysical nature. Go ahead – *try* to explain it to your friends and relatives. They will smile politely, squirm uncomfortably, and eventually they will stop returning your phone calls and look the other way when they see you coming. And who can blame them? They live in the real world with their office jobs and nuclear families and a host of mindless sitcoms waiting on the propaganda box at the end of their busy day. In direct contrast, it could be observed that anyone who has dedicated

4

themselves to the pursuit of forbidden knowledge really doesn't live in that world at all. Not for lack of wanting, perhaps, but because the real world is quickly seen to be little more than a series of programs and illusions – not unlike *The Matrix*. To the seeker who diligently unravels the programs which have been put onto her since birth, the "real world" becomes less and less real, but instead a tangled web of false belief systems and erroneous conclusions. And not surprisingly, the people who populate that world may begin to take on a peculiar zombie-like quality – actors on a hidden stage which is built and reinforced with every thought, motion and action.

What this ultimately means is that the seeker finds herself alone in a vast world of illusions – and I've found that it was, for me, the *only* state from which I could begin to seriously test the knowledge I had gleaned from Orlando during those six years of immersion – what I have called at times my baptism in the River Styx. It *is* like dying in a way. All the seeker had thought to be true turns out to be false, and much of what was thought to be false turns out to be true. The world turns upside down, and in the process, the seeker finds herself compiling what amounts to a grimoire focused on the fundamental question: *Who am I, and what exists beyond the ability of my five physical senses to detect?* The seeker says to herself, "I acknowledge that the world is nothing like I was taught to believe, so... what *is* it and where do I fit in the grand equation?"

In order to explore that question to its depths, and in response to Orlando tossing me out of the comfort zone of that cosmic classroom, I launched the Quantum Shaman™ website in the year 2000, and opened my first interactive discussion forum as a means to test the cohesion of my own assimilation by slamming everything I had learned against the physical world, the metaphysical world, and the world of quantum consciousness.

This process lasted in earnest for approximately five years – even though it continued well beyond that timeframe and still does to a certain extent, to this day – spring, 2012 at the time of this writing. It's an ongoing process, an interactive evolution. But in hindsight, I would have to say that if the cosmic classroom (1994-2000) was an intensive crash course in enlightenment and the awakening of awareness, then the years between 2000-2005 were an extended experiment in assimilating cohesion, putting together the oddly shaped pieces of the puzzle of the Self.

And then, one fine day, I realized I was done with it. I had slammed my knowledge against the real world and it remained unbroken. Not faith-based, but rooted in experiences. What I had discovered – in a neat little nutshell – was that the thing that survives beyond this physical life is what shamans and mystics call the double, or the Other. Not just in some mystical manner of a mysterious overlord, but in the manifestation of one's Totality. Simply put, the totality of oneself might be best described as everything we have learned in *this* lifetime, combined with the *conscious awareness* of everything one has learned in all our other manifestations – most of which we cannot entirely wrap our minds around from our humanform perspective.

With that said, I do not believe for a single moment in reincarnation as it is commonly interpreted. What most humans think of as reincarnation is actually a movement of the Other within the bendable fabric of the Now. In quantum terms, it might be said that the Other can be in many locations at once (non-local), or more precisely, the Other represents what I have come to call the super-position of the Self, or in Toltec terms, the super-position of the **assemblage point**[1]. If we were to encounter our Other in the year 1912, for example,

[1] Items in bold underline may be found in the glossary at the back of this book. The glossary also appears on the Quantum Shaman website for your convenience.

we might find him on board _Titanic_ as she was sinking into the murky depths of the North Atlantic. Encounter him at another point in time – 1492, just for example – and perhaps you would find the Other deep inside the walls of the Vatican, attempting to make sense of The Pope's strange behaviors. Confront him in the year 1969, and you might find yourself walking on the moon or dancing in the rain at Woodstock. Ultimately, the Other is the highest aspect of the Self, existing _as_ the totality even _before_ the seeker – the mortal source of all of it - takes her first step on the path. And yet, the Other is wholly and absolutely the creation _of_ the mortal self, without whom the Other could not exist.

How is this possible? Because time itself is the greatest illusion of all. Rather than attempt to explain that statement here, suffice to say that time is not the linear process we generally think. For anyone who has looked into the nature of time, even from a layman's perspective, it is quickly recognized that we create time as a sorting tool, but time in and of itself doesn't appear to exist as an extant force of nature.

Regardless of time, space and the effects of gravity on gophers, it was 2005 when I first shook myself off and went back to that cosmic classroom to report my progress – my successes and failures, my comments and observations. I had just completed my first book in the _Quantum Shaman_™ series – _Diary of a Nagual Woman_ - and so it stands to reason, it was _also_ in 2005 when Orlando gave me one of those looks that only an evolved but presently non-local being can give, and said... "It's not your neatly typed essays that interest me, but the scrawls on the walls of your soul."

I stood there in the realm of hypothetical space/time for an eternity, listening to the echo of those words ringing in my ears. And as a result, I spent the _next_ six years assimilating the assimilation – a work which Orlando referred to as gathering the cohesion of the dark enlightenment.

What follows in these pages is the result of that process. Some of these words fell onto the pages of my journal. Others were written to friends and apprentices around the world. Still others came from dialogues on my online forums: *The Shaman's Rattle* and *The Sorcerer's World*. Some of it may amuse you. Some of it may shock you. But as the old cliché goes: *if you're not outraged, you're not paying attention.*

These are the scrawls on the walls of my soul.

Della Van Hise
Yucca Valley, California
Spring, 2012

Death creates itself,
given Time.

A word to the wise. . .

If you are fearful of having your current foundation rattled, go no further. If you are angry at the world, leave your anger at the door. If you are only looking for validation of existing belief systems, you are welcome here, but remember that once you see the world as it is, there will be no going back to the comfortable world of illusions.

This is a place for those who are interested in seriously examining programs and confronting their belief systems, shaking their foundations to the core, and gazing deep into the eyes of their own infinite self.

Nothing is what you have been taught to believe.

———

Part One

Assimilating the Self

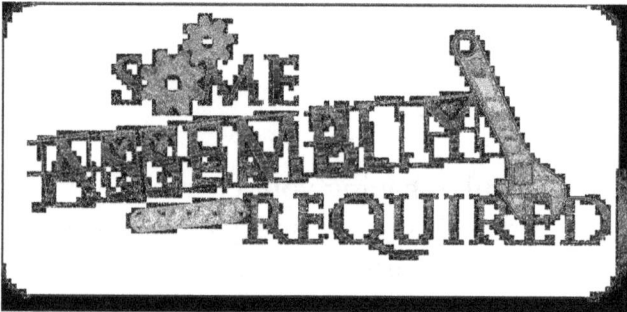

When someone asks who you are, they generally want to know your name, whether you're married or single, and if you might sleep with them. Or maybe they're just being polite and really don't give a damn. Most likely that's the case. But let's assume for a moment that *you* really want to answer the question – "Who am I?"

Where do you look for answers?

The obvious answer is too obvious: Look inside yourself, young Grasshopper.

And yet... how do you look inside yourself if you don't know who you are?

Ain't *that* annoying?

Metanoia and Personal Cohesion
How do you find yourself if you don't know who you are?

August 8, 2010

In a **gnosis** session with **Orlando**, the subject was raised, "Why do apprentices fail?" Put another way, why do some seem on the verge of enlightenment and self-awakening, only to abandon their path and return to the **consensual agreement** in the same way that dude returned to the matrix for nothing more than a juicy steak?

In essence, someone on a path toward enlightenment or spiritual evolution goes through a period of approximately 2-5 years wherein they are required (by their own intent) to strip away false personalities, make contact with the authentic self, and literally fall in love with the whole *thing*. It can be any *thing*, but at some level, the *thing* will be what amounts to the muse of one's path. Maybe a book you once read. Maybe a beloved fairy tale half-remembered from childhood. Maybe some movie that stirs one's heart and awakens the universal questions: "Who am I?" "What is my purpose in the universe?" "Is there anything beyond this life?"

Whatever the *thing* itself, it is always a catalyst that stimulates the brain/mind into an almost spontaneous awakening, and there the journey really begins. In my own experience, the *thing* first gave me a glimpse of itself at age 6, when I happened to be in the living room and caught a glimpse of Gardner McKay from the old television series, *Adventures In Paradise*. Later on, the *thing* evolved to encompass the *Star Trek* character of Mr. Spock – the stoic but

11

inwardly-conflicted Vulcan, the half-alien among humans, the essence of sanity in the midst of what was usually abject madness and the quantifiable distraction of scantily-clad women.

Over the years, the muse has continued to evolve until, finally, it has taken the form of the Other or the **double** – the **totality** of myself. This seems to be the general process – but it is the falling-in-love-obsession that comes first, and leads eventually to the assimilation of one's personal **cohesion** – when all of those aspects of the Self turn and embrace one another, becoming a gestalt comprised of the mortal self (the source), the various avatars one wears in the course of a billion manifestations, and the cohesive yet virtually inexplicable Other which will serve as the vessel of awareness and continuity beyond this peculiar interval we call Life.

During that initial awakening, the apprentice hopefully goes through a process called **metanoia** - which Joseph Chilton Pearce (*The Crack In The Cosmic Egg*) describes as what occurs when the student is seized with the essence of the *thing* itself. Pearce uses the example of physics, saying that any competent student may become a physicist, but only a rare few will become so possessed by the *spirit* of physics that they *become* an extension of the thing itself. Those few will go on to be the great forward thinkers – Einstein, Hawking, Schroedinger, Sheldon Cooper, just to name a few – the ones who change the world as a result of their metanoia.

The bottom line here is rather harsh, but true. One cannot rationally or logically *choose* to be overcome with a metanoia of spirit. While the techniques of quantum shamanism™ or spiritual enlightenment can be studied, the metanoia either seizes the apprentice or it doesn't. Those who are seized become compelled to *do* the thing and nothing can dissuade them from their path. Those who aren't seized can certainly reach enlightenment, spiritual evolution and a position of heightened awareness, but chances are they will be much more settled and integrated into the world of matter and men. Put simply: those who are seized with a true metanoia may not ever return to any sort of ordinary awareness again – which can be both beneficial and disastrous. They become the modern-day shamans and visionaries, the seers and the dream-weavers, and yet many would tell you it is not a life they might have chosen, because the path is neither selective nor forgiving. Give yourself to it, and it will take all you have and change you forever – for that is the ultimate definition of evolution.

According to most self-help gurus and self-appointed experts, this process of enlightenment may take decades and cost thousands upon thousands of dollars. If you believe that, there's a bridge in Brooklyn I'll sell you for cheap! Enlightenment really doesn't take a lifetime – and it is entirely free for those who are guided by their own double, their own inner teacher. For anyone seriously devoted to the process, it takes a few years at most to actually strip away the bullshit of the consensus reality, open one's eyes outside the box, and realize that one is now fundamentally different than the other humans with whom s/he shares the third rock from the sun. Not better. Not worse. Just different – mainly with regard to how one views the world and their place within it. Those who inhabit the assemblage point of the authentic self find themselves surprisingly awake in a world that is asleep, surrounded by organic puppets still dangling from the strings of the consensual agreement.

While the Other possesses the ability to move outside the space/time continuum, accumulating the experience we mistakenly think of as past lives, the mortal self is charged with the task of assimilating all those aspects of the Self and –

somehow – bringing them together in such a way as to inhabit the totality of the Self. *That* is the *process* of spiritual evolution – the assimilation of all that we are into a single point of awareness wherein we would have total recall of all those other aspects of the Self.

It's the "somehow" where things start to get interesting – the process of interacting with the Other through the vehicle of gnosis (silent knowing). In the initial stages, the connection between mortal self and immortal Other may seem tenuous, uncertain. But as with anything, the more often one engages the process, the more proficient one becomes. You won't even go blind or grow hair on your palms.

But it's also as Yoda said: "Do, or do not. There is no try." While you're hanging around with your friends waiting for enlightenment to find you, life is going by, faster and faster with every day one is alive. All too soon, it's over and there are no do-overs, no curtain calls, no instant replays, despite what your friendly priest, pastor or guru may have told you. There is only Now. Squander it and it's lost forever.

So, what takes *this* lifetime is the *realization* of spiritual evolution – the transformation from human to higher self. If you plan on waiting for your *next* lifetime, what makes you think there will be one? What makes you believe there will be a tomorrow? Is it possible that a lot of what we believe has no basis in reality whatsoever? Or, more precisely, that what we believe has been so weighed down with erroneous conclusions that the thing itself has become skewed or even lost in the shuffle?

In trying to illustrate this, I like the story of the Martian who comes to Earth and lands at the garbage dump. He sees mountains of garbage and a swarming sea of flies. The Martian has one of those light bulb moments and loudly proclaims, "Isn't it amazing how these flies have created all this garbage!"

Erroneous conclusions – the stock in trade for most **belief systems**. Once they take hold, getting rid of them is about as easy as getting rid of crabs. Best to not go there in the first place – which involves, in this case, a keen awareness of the difference between what we believe and what we actually know.

During the process of enlightenment and awakening, one is coached by her mentor, whether an extant teacher or one's own higher self. This is a period of great excitement, a sense of accomplishment, and a time when the cosmic downloads were coming so fast that I could not record them all. During my own period of metanoia (1995-2000, roughly), I composed the equivalent of 10+ full-length novels in my journal. Granted, not all of it is profound, but some of it *is* - at least with regard to my personal view and experience of the multiverse, as well as the potential comprehension of the quantum machinations of energy at the level where one might actually possess the ability to achieve **transmogrification, transformation** and **transcendence**.

During the period of metanoia, one is on top of the world. But eventually, almost unnoticed by the apprentice, the teacher/mentor takes a step back. The support system is cleverly removed - and it is then that the apprentice must learn to hold that state of enlightenment together on her own, without the constant input from the teacher. This is the process of learning to be cohesive from within. And yet, when the teacher *does* take that step back, the apprentice may find herself feeling lost, adrift, even bereft.

This is the point at which many apprentices fail, or at least falter. And, of course, it has a tremendous connection to the whole idea of the consensus reality - without a consensus, most humans simply are not able to maintain their own individual beliefs and practices. Sounds simple... and it is. And yet, the important thing is to examine this idea in our own lives. To what extent are you cohesive and whole when you are a universe of one? Who are you when no one else is looking?

Of course, this can get into a discussion about why humans are so compelled to form agreements. What is it that appears to make us *need* others to agree with us, particularly on issues of religion, god, political views and the like? And where does the instinct come from which essentially says, "Kill the heretic!" when someone *doesn't* agree with one of those existing belief systems? What can be done to strengthen one's individual cohesion to the point that no extant agreement or support system is required?

So we enter into act two – wherein we must not only identify the authentic Self, but make peace with it, and ultimately breathe into it the ability to *Be* itself even when no outside validation exists.

"The only gods that exist
are those who are perpetually self-creating."
(Orlando – 2012)

Amazing Grace
Forgive me for asking, but are we really wretches, m'lord?

> *I am disturbed when I look at people around me. I get the sense that the whole human race believes they are worth nothing! It is maddening! It's as if all our worth gets transferred from who we <u>are</u> to the <u>idea</u> of who we are... which really <u>is</u> worthless.*

I used to have more of a problem with other people than I do now. Took me years to realize one minor detail. They, too, have a choice. And it is their choices that make them believe whatever it is they believe - whether the belief that they are worthless, or the belief that the sky tyrant is going to take time out to listen to their prayers, when it's often actually the belief in the sky tyrant that makes them think they're worthless in the first place. The lyrics to *Amazing Grace* have always troubled me... "Amazing Grace, that saved a wretch like me."

So many people go through life with that mindset. They are wretches needing to be saved from something, when the reality is that if they would simply *choose* not to be wretches in the first place, they would no longer need saving from anything – except their own false belief systems. The problem with most organized religions is that they are self-serving and incestuous. If all the true believers were schooled to use their *own* abilities and their *own* wits, the church would be out of business. For that reason, organized religion actively encourages people to see themselves as wretches – after all, that's what keeps them coming back to the stained glass shack to put their pennies in the collection plate and sing songs to the sky tyrant in the insane hope that it will take pity on them and spare them from... what? Death? Taxes? Seems unlikely. People have been praying since the dawn of time, and as far as I know they are still dying and still emptying their pockets every April 15. Either God is deaf or simply doesn't give a damn. We're on our own down here on Planet Earth, and that would be perfectly all right if only we (as a species) could start using that incredible computer sitting on the top of our shoulders for something *other* than war, watching the tube, and other forms of self-mutilating masturbation.

The truly ironic thing about most organized religions is that they actively discourage their followers from using the abilities with which we are clearly born. Intuition and spontaneous awareness (silent knowing) are said to be "of the devil." Put another way, we are taught that our inner bullshit detectors are from the dark side because in *most* cases, they really *do* detect the bullshit and expose the bullshitters, and so it stands to reason that the biggest bullshitters have the biggest investment in keeping the sheeple ignorant and scared. When the human organism is programmed to reject one of its primary senses, the good guys have become the bad guys and the dark side wins. Cue the Darth Vader fanfare and launch the TIE fighters.

After all, within the framework of the organization itself, the church is the only sanctioned teacher – yet as we all know, incest leads to imbeciles, and that's where it all starts to break down in ways most people won't even dare to look at. I know folks who send their kids to private Christian schools, and the kids hit the streets at the age of 17 or 18, not knowing a condom from a cracker jack, because there seems to be some notion that ignoring reality will make it go away. Instead, the end result is a self-fulfilling prophecy created by fear and ignorance itself: pregnant teenagers who then try to tell their horrified parents that it's the second immaculate conception. Fear and ignorance have been instilled into us by those who pretend to be the gateway to our salvation. It would be downright funny if it weren't so tragic.

Prayer. What is it? For some people, it's a long list of regrets and demands whispered into the pillow just prior to sleep. "Dear God: Please forgive me for all those naughty fantasies about that girl in my biology class, and if you could see your way clear, I'd really like a new Mustang for my birthday instead of the usual socks and underwear. Amen." Something like that. "Oh, yeah, and while you're at it, please keep an eye on mom and dad." But you know you said that last part because it made you look good, and not because you really meant it.

For others, prayer is mostly mumbling over the meat. "Good bread, good meat, good God, let's eat!" Sure, it's good to be thankful, but why not thank the spirit of the cow who gave up her life so you could have that rib eye? Why not thank the farmer who busted his junk to grow the wheat to make the bread? Think about what you're saying. Think about what you're doing. Think about *why* you are thinking it and doing it! That's the first step toward enlightenment! Stop being a robot going through the motions of who you think you *should* be, and ask yourself for a moment what you *really* think about all the nonsense in your life that ceases to make *any* sense when you stop and really *think* about it!

Some have accused me of being a foul-tempered little atheist. Not really. I have an absolute Knowledge that there are things we do not and cannot understand. Sometimes I call it Spirit – or what George Lucas referred to as "the Force." Doesn't mean it's sentient in and of itself. Doesn't mean it gives a damn. What it *might* mean is that there is some quantifiable something that we can connect with on our journey – *without* having to ask it for blessings or forgiveness or salvation or a bigger TV than the asshole next door.

> Intent is the unwavering image held in the heart of your heart and soul - the paradigm upon which everything you Think or Do becomes a Realized reflection of the paradigm itself. It is a meta-physical part of you, invisible to the naked eye but no less real than liver or spleen, and if you aren't using it to its full potential, your evolving self is incomplete, dis-eased as a body without a heart, see?

Intent is the active side of clarity, an unwavering vision held firmly in the mind, which serves as the seeker's direct interface between question and answer; the metamagickal probe or prod applied to the all-knowing All as a means of extracting the specific Knowledge required to achieve the manifestation of the intent itself; it is the quantum questioning mother of the Will - *not* the Will, but without which the Will can never manifest because without Intent the Will has nothing *to* manifest, nothing to create, no seed to nurture; Intent is the goal/vision the seeker projects unceasingly onto the silent screen of eternity until eternity reflects the seeker's will by yielding up the information required to achieve the Intended evolution. Intent does not compromise. It does not yield to reason or common sense. It can be summoned clearly, instantly and impeccably in all states of awareness by invocation of the word Intent.

Orlando – November 23, 1999

So if prayer is little more than mumbling over the meat, Intent is the phenomenal force at the core of all acts of creation.

Why am I harping on god and religion? Because at the core of human experience, and particularly in our various world cultures, the concepts of god and religion shape who and what we are even more than politics or cultural pressures – and it is only by confronting those age-old programs that we are able to strip away the false beliefs that hold us prisoner to the consensus itself.

If you want to believe in god or if you are deeply enmeshed in your religion, that's perfectly okay. It's a good social outlet. But it won't help you with your spiritual evolution (because The Program itself doesn't allow for that), and it won't save you from death and taxes. Kinda like Santa Claus. Fun to fantasize, but do let me know when you actually see Fat Boy squeezing his big red butt down the chimney. Then I'll become a believer.

Pray for your limitations and they are yours. No deity required. Just simple math.

Immortal drums play in the night,
irregular heartbeats
a satyr's hoofbeats
Echoing off the black leather skin
stretched taut over the lips
of the abyss.

On the Trail of the Authentic Self
"I found myself, but some of the pieces are missing!"

January, 2012

Perhaps one of the most difficult aspects of manifesting the **authentic self** is getting outside the box of the consensual agreement. This, in turn, raises an interesting question: why _do_ we need others to agree with us? Why have so many wars been fought in the name of gods, politics and cultural ideology if we are solitary creatures?

The simple answer lies in what Carlos Castaneda referred to as **the foreign installation**, or what the Wachowski Brothers brought into pop culture as *The Matrix*. If you read nothing else from the glossary, take a moment to look to look at the entry entitled "foreign installation", because until the seeker has a firm understanding not only of *what* the FI is, but the absolute awareness *that it exists at all*, s/he may be operating under the fanciful delusion that her thoughts and behaviors are entirely her own.

They aren't.

The foreign installation is what I have come to call The Program or the **overlay** – quite literally an operating system that is laid down onto the hard drive of the brain in the same manner Windows or Linux or DOS give a computer its basic sense of structure. It has elements of Jung's collective unconscious, but that's just the tip of the iceberg. What *is* The Program? Basically it is the shoulds and shouldn'ts, the rules and regulations, and most of all the belief systems of the consensual reality. Put another way, The Program is the basic operating system under which all humans function until such time as they realize they are being controlled and manipulated by a paradigm which is not their own, and whose sole intent is to ultimately kill them.

Where does The Program come from? It comes from all of us – but to get a little more specific, think back to when you were a very young child. Many can't remember anything before the age of 5 or 6, and there's a reason. Prior to that, we exist in a state of the authentic self. We have not yet been assimilated into the society that will eventually swallow us. Prior to that so-called age-of-reason (normally between 5-7 years of age) we are more or less strangers in a strange land, living in an idyllic but at times peculiar reality.

As we begin to be absorbed into the larger consensus, we are forced to adopt *its* rules and belief systems because we are told by those we trust (normally our parents or care-givers) that "This is just how it's done, kid! We eat meat and potatoes for dinner, we pretend not to notice that Grandma smells like stale urine and has an oozing wart on her nose, we work to pay for the car we need to drive to work to pay for the car, and we go to church on Sundays to pray to the sky tyrant to deliver us from the temptations he put in front of us, and forgive us for being the wretches he created us to be. Any questions?"

I had lots of questions. None of it made any sense. Nor should it. Our societies and individual cultures do the things they do not because they are rational, but often because it's just the way things have always been done, and unless we wake up and start to *see* that the merry-go-round is spinning of control and flew off its axis long ago, we spend the rest of our lives going through the motions of trying to play by a series of rules and beliefs which have absolutely *nothing* to do with the authentic self, and even less to do with any notion of Reality.

Do I believe the foreign installation is sentient or sinister? Many do, but I personally don't see it that way. It's just a program created by the consensus - but it is a deadly one because it will always adhere to the lowest common denominator of thought-less (i.e. "automaton") behavior, and it will shout in our ear from dusk to dawn that we are worthless, brainless, witless, junkless and stupid. And it will convince us that we are fated to die, when the reality of that may be very different for those who take the time and energy to overcome The Program itself.

Many see the foreign installation as a conscious or even extraterrestrial force, but it's just the drone of the consensus on auto-pilot, with no sentient force at the helm. It's doing what it was programmed to do - to thwart human evolution - largely because the universe has built-in default programs whose sole function is to do just that: thwart human evolution. *Why?* Because if it were easy, if it were a straightforward path to an easily-seen goal, it would not be evolution, but only a walk in the park. *The foreign installation is the device that challenges us to evolve beyond the challenge itself.*

It is an extension of the humanform wavelength - the mechanism we have built to distract ourselves, test ourselves, thwart ourselves, and trap ourselves, unless and until we turn around, look ourselves in the eye, and say, "Hey, is this what you really want, or are you just running this program by default? Do you believe the crap you're singing to yourself in your internal dialog or can you see it's all just a meaningless chant spun into being by your scared little-self?"

When we have the wherewithal to *see* the foreign installation for the Agent Smith it is, we open ourselves to the power which will enable us to defeat it. What is that power? Simply put: it is the power of surrender. Surrender to whom? To the higher self, the dreaming self, the double - the self who exists outside of The Program. When you finally surrender is the moment when the Other begins dreaming you into being and instructing you from within, and therefore you are no longer controlled by The Program.

The only cure for the foreign installation is awareness of the dis-ease. Once a seeker begins to really see that so much of what we believe is the result of cultural and social programming, we embrace the ability to have a keen awareness of everything we think, do, believe. That's the nature of self-*stalking* - questioning not only our own beliefs, but *why* we believe the things we do, where those beliefs come from, and finally asking ourselves if they have *any* veracity whatsoever. Most don't. Most are just mumblings of the foreign installation whispering in our ear through the internal dialog.

Armed with that awareness, we can begin to step outside the foreign installation's commands and take back our own autonomy.

I knocked myself unconscious
on the edge of human consciousness.
Perhaps a paradox
should have the manners to announce itself
before it knows it's coming.

A Solitary Path

April 7, 2009

When I talk about this being a solitary journey, I mean it is precisely that when push comes to shove, when thinking turns to do-ing. While it's possible to work in groups for learning techniques or honing practices, the part of the journey that will lead to real freedom isn't anything that any extant teacher is going to be able to show us - because, ultimately, what leads to real freedom is the wholeness of the authentic self - the integrated, self-aware being who has amassed her cohesion above and beyond any and all teachers, friends, family. And let's face it - teachers can be a positive influence, but they can also become dependencies, and that is especially true in spiritual circles where the stakes are literally life and death. So it seems to me that when we turn and face the ultimate truth, it tends to read in big red letters, "You are alone." (And in smaller letters: "And that's okay!")

I realize this may not be what many want to hear. That's okay - I completely understand the need for a sense of unity and the draw of what Carlos Castaneda referred to as "the warrior's party". Nothing wrong with that. A lot of good can come of it, but also a lot of harm – such as what occurred in Castaneda's final years on Earth and the "cult" that sprang up around him.

Where I find myself questioning is when it is put forth that we *must* have an extant teacher, or we *must* work as a group if we are to achieve freedom. On the one hand, it sounds good. But on the other hand, what does that really look like? What can you do for me, or what can I do for you that will bring you one step closer to your freedom? Food for thought. Is there some knowledge I possess that might advance your journey? If so, you have only to ask and I will attempt to impart it. Is there some bit of magic or gem of experience that might help me to unlock the secret to transformation? If so, please contact me so that we might put our heads together.

Sometimes I see the idea of groups not unlike the old biblical tale of the tower of Babel. You have a bunch of people working together to build a stairway to heaven, but it's thwarted because all of them end up speaking different languages, and so the project gets scrapped because suddenly nobody can understand one another. Words get in the way - and so do egos, agendas and personalities. Sure, we can work with awareness to overcome some of those elements, but do we really ever overthrow them, or do we just mask them for a time until they figure out some other way to resurface?

No amount of shouting from the rafters or rattling of swords is going to make one bit of difference with anyone else – whether in a seminar or an online discussion group. Others may hear you and may even agree with you, but ultimately the visions we are given during these experiences are entirely our own. Solitary. What I've had to internalize and integrate in my own journey is the awareness that no matter how much I may *see* "the path", no matter how much I may understand the double, no matter how much knowledge I have amassed in my journey... its relevance is almost 100% to myself alone. There we go again... the solitary journey. Maybe something I say may help someone else clarify something, or maybe it only befuddles them all the more. Who's to say?

The only reason to do any of this is for our own assimilation. That's the purpose of tales of power – to inspire, to motivate, and to help us define our own authentic self as we see it reflected back at us through the stories which go to make up our lives. We go through phases where we want to share our knowledge with others, because we do genuinely want them to feel that grand love affair with the infinite - that incredible, heart-bursting, phenomenally life-altering union we share with our own double. We want others to share in our joy and our wonder and our bliss.

And yet...

We have to be careful not to become evangelical. Nothing more off-putting than some newly-saved born-againer trying to sell us his god and scare us out of his hell. Even in spiritual circles, the same kind of thing can happen if we're not careful. We know how clearly *we* see something, and if only the rest of the world could see it, too, then everything would be right and good. What that boils down to is a desire to form a new consensus, a new agreement. And, of course, any consensus will eventually rob the seeker of her authentic self, and so, again, we must acknowledge that this is a solitary path, shared only by the self and the Other.

If we ever caught the muse and were able to share him with our neighbor, the magical part of the journey would be over, and we would no longer feel the need to struggle toward that elusive state which we call freedom.

We may benefit intellectually, emotionally and even as a sense of physical well-being from our work with groups or teachers; but the real quest for freedom is where we find ourselves solo. We go off into the unknown to gain experience, then come together to share tales of power by the cyberfire. And from that, if we are fortunate, perhaps we gain the inspiration and strength to venture again into the unknown... alone.

Freedom is attained when we no longer have any need to return to the fire, when we become the flame that lights our own path.

Candles keep journals
of time's passing
in empty books of matches.

Recapitulating God

2 a.m. and the wind is soft and silver, a night-blanket cut from stardust and smoke from the fires in other people's chimneys. I climb the little knoll across the street and study the world as if it is a book written on the fabric of the universe - yet it is a book whose pages are forever changing in the same way dreams bend and quiver when one tries to look at them too closely. Nothing remains the same, yet everything is eternal in the Now. Perhaps that is all that can be said of the Infinite.

Gazing back in the direction of my house, I wonder if I am sleeping peacefully in my own bed, dreaming myself out here in the lonesome desert where the coyotes are prowling ever closer and the mockingbird is restless and off-key. Even the moon is a broken egg, lop-sided and bleeding albumen clouds that linger for only a moment before they are gone, like shapeless phantoms moving in and out of the night.

There was a time long ago when I wanted to believe in God. That is the thought that comes to me, uninvited. Just the prattle of the internal dialog running its inventory of the past. And so for a moment I am 7 years old again, trying on the role playing game of faith in some old man with a long grey beard sitting on a celestial throne. But in my heart, even then, I knew there was no God, just as I knew there was no Santa, no Easter bunny, no goddess or guru who could give me the keys to heaven. There is only the Self in its many manifestations - the mortal self, the immortal Other, the eternal I-Am who is the cohesion of both. Just those three... my personal triumvirate. And, of course, all the identities and manifestations the Other puts on in order to learn the lessons required to teach the mortal self the process of its own evolution. A billion or so past lives that aren't really 'past' at all, but more like stories in a long book of fairy tales, with each and every character being one more Self, all of whom will turn out to be the storyteller when all is said and done.

It's enough to make my heads spin.

How very much easier it all would have been if only I could have believed in God. And yet... belief is not for warriors, and gods have no place in the Infinite. In recapitulating our gods, we give up our faith in external sources of salvation, turning instead to a one-on-one interpersonal relationship with eternity.

A Joshua tree scratches the wind with skeletal fingers, causing the night to sing softly to itself, like an old man whistling past a graveyard where his own tombstone already stands waiting with the date of his birth inscribed, and the date of his death drawing ever closer to the marble.

Overhead, a shooting star seems to hesitate in flight, perhaps just long enough to recapitulate the fall from heaven, the destruction of faith that paves the way for evolution. "As long as god exists, you are working with a safety net." So says the Silence in the middle of the night.

Alone in the darkness, we shed our gods in order to embrace the god-force of Creation within.

Role-Playing and Self-Stalking
This Ain't the Oscars and You Ain't Al Pacino

August 26, 2008

One of the hardest tasks we face as warriors and seekers involves coming face to face with the characters we play in our day to day lives. The entire issue of role-playing has to do with survival in the human world, but survival often comes at a great price. People who adopt roles *without* awareness usually find themselves in a heap of misery, because the role and reality usually don't go hand in hand. For example, I know a woman who plays the role of The Good Wife. With that comes certain "responsibilities" (her word). She must cook the husband's meals, do his laundry, fold his socks, perform her wifely duties twice a week upon request. And all of this must be done with a smile, even though said husband has been cheating on her for years, abuses her verbally, and married her to be a maid rather than a companion.

The problem is that she has no awareness of any of this because the role of The Good Wife has blinded her to what's going on all around her. Actors on Broadway who perform the same role for years have reported that eventually they start to lose the boundary between themselves and their character, and surely the same is true for humans in general. Live the lie long enough, and eventually the lie is all there is.

A seeker may adopt a role, but it is always done with awareness. This is the art of stalking as it was put forth by Carlos Castaneda. For example, there have been times at one of our events when I will quite happily play the role of The Dumb Blonde, because most customers are less intimidated by The Dumb Blonde than by the real essence of who-I-am. Easiest way to explain it - when someone is looking at an expensive ring, and asks me, "So, how are you doing today?" my response is going to be what the person wants/needs to hear. "I'm great! You?" Chat them up, but never on anything too heavy unless they open that door first – which does happen on occasion. But in most cases, if I answered their questions truthfully, they would flee in terror.

It might look something like this:

"How are you doing today?" Joe Bloke asks, but has no real interest in the answer. Just polite conversation, small-talk, bullshit to pass the time. This is his role.

The *honest* response might be...

"Well, lemme see, Joe. We are, in theory, beings who are going to die, and short of taking responsibility for every moment we are alive, we will most likely fall into the abyss, experiencing the absolute annihilation of any awareness we ever possessed. The planet herself is in stage 4 terminal cancer and may be knocked out of orbit at any moment by a rogue comet, but other than that, I'm having a great day. You?"

All true, but inappropriate for the circumstances. So the stalker puts on her mask, plays her role, but always with the total knowledge that the mask is not the self. It is a tool – a survival mechanism. And yet, the moment we forget it's a tool, we run the same risk as anyone else.

This is the danger of folly. If you were to assume the role of happy caroler, singing phantom songs beneath a frosted window on Christmas Eve, the danger is that you would start to believe it is real. This is what it means to be a phantom – continually trying on new clothes and new roles, believing them for a time then abandoning them in favor of some new cloak handed down to you from mother or father, sister or brother. Yes, it is true that you can fake it till you make it, but when you forget you are faking it, what you have actually made is your own graveyard bed.

Under no circumstances is it acceptable to put on the mask of a phantom, for all too often, what you do not realize is that the phantoms have lined the mask with glue that is anesthesia and pleasant amnesia.

(Orlando – August, 2001)

A stalker chooses his/her role from the perspective of being fully awake, whereas the ordinary man walks through life in that state of pleasant amnesia, in a series of roles that are not of his choosing. At work, he is The Successful Businessman (which demands a certain uniform of his trade, whether coveralls or Armani suit, just as an actor dons the trappings of his character). At home, he is The Loving Husband (a different set of clothes). With the kiddies, he is The Attentive Father (replete with football jersey and feigned interest in the yearly science project).

Problem is... if none of those roles are talking to one another through a cohesive I-Am, there is a tendency to fragment and eventually one ends up on anti-depressants, because each role comes with a whole set of expectations. The successful business man *expects* that promotion, which may instead be given to a junior partner who is less deserving, but happens to be the boss's nephew. The loving husband *expects* a loving wife in return, but may come to realize that because he was playing a role and not really operating from the platform of his authentic self, his wife lost interest in him years ago and the entire marriage is nothing more than a fragile illusion. The attentive father *expects* his kids to do well in school, but will be dismayed to discover that they are selling meth to the first graders for reasons that may not ever be clear, but probably have to do with having received too many mixed messages from too many role-players.

For the advanced seeker, there is always a keen awareness of whatever role we may be playing at any given time. I am well aware when I am playing the role of The Bitch in order to stalk some aspect of myself. To others, I may appear mad as a shithouse mouse, but beneath the spinning, churning Tasmanian devil is the cohesive self who is essentially the director/writer of *all* the roles. That's the difference between the seeker and the ordinary man. The seeker projects from the authentic self at all times, whereas the ordinary man, with his beliefs and expectations, with his costume changes and lines to memorize, has no real idea that there is an authentic self at all, because he becomes caught up in each and every role to such an extent that it becomes his sole reality. He loses his identity and becomes a conduit for whatever character he may be playing from moment to moment.

So what? "What does that have to do with *me*?" you ask.

Next time you find yourself in an intense situation – whether at work, with a spouse or children, or arguing vehemently for your own point of view, stop for a moment and listen to your **internal dialog**. You will probably hear the voice of your character. You may even see him in his super hero costume, arguing for truth, justice and the American Way.

Grab the nearest gun. Shoot the fucker. Then run like hell off the stage and out of the play.

The authentic self is the one standing in the shadows, waiting for you to wake up. No capes or masks. No magical weapons. No special abilities.

Except one.

The authentic self is the most powerful being in the universe, because from the cohesive assemblage point of the authentic self, there is *nothing* you cannot do.

Raven wings blow the darkness aside,
brushing the sky with dawn.
The shaman haunts adobe ruins,
seeking ghosts of old miners
to ask their counsel on life and death.
October wind blows cold yellow daylight,
whispering with certainty
that all the spirits are dead,
their only afterlife a dim reflection
fading in the mirrored memories of mortals.
Nearby, stones spell out a message,
black rock on pale sand:
I AM.

Forbidden Fruit
Pay no attention to that ally behind the curtain!

Stardate Unknown
~circa 2001

I once had a seeker say to me, "But Della, everything you've ever said is now suspect because we know you took drugs to get your result!"

Drugs? Never took drugs. Journeyed with the mushroom ally a few times – but the allies are hardly "drugs" in any conventional sense, though I'm sure there are those who will choose to argue even though they have no experience with the allies. Some people just enjoy conflict, or have become the voice of Agent Smith, whether they ever realize it or not.

If I have a raging infection, I might go to a doctor to get antibiotics in order to overcome a sickness that is debilitating and perhaps even deadly. It's no different with our perceptions. We are sick to our souls. It's why depression, murder, suicide, bipolar disorder are so prevalent in the world today. There's something intrinsically wrong with us down to a cellular level, and when push comes to shove, when patients and doctors get real with one another, the bottom line of most depression is directly related to awareness of one's own mortality. This can include grief over the loss of a loved one, nebulous fears, panic attacks, illness and the like. We know we will die and return to the dust unless there is some miraculous intervention, but the old myths of miracles don't hold water. We don't really believe in the old gods, and yet we sense there is something magickal within us that could transcend death… if only we knew how. But because our current Western society is designed in such a way as to prohibit us from going on that journey of self-discovery, we have become sick-to-the-soul as a species, and languish in the pharmacopoeia of prescription pain killers for the soul, which are little more than slave collars of obedience to numb us to the very pain that should be driving us to look for real answers instead of only feel-good placeboes.

It isn't our bodies that are sick, but our minds. Our perceptions. And so, as shamans around the world have known since the dawn of time, one way to begin healing our perceptions is to strip away that social and cultural sickness. Unfortunately, in most cases, the things that make us sick are so deeply imbedded into our programming that most of us are unable to do that stripping away on our own. Fortunately, nature has provided us with what is undoubtedly the legendary, mythical "forbidden fruit", and it comes in the form of a mushroom which can go a long way toward curing us of the programs that make us so culturally and spiritually sick.

Know this: I am not advocating the use of mushrooms or any other "drug", even though my personal opinion is that we would live in a much more well-balanced world if every human being were required to experience the mushroom journey at least once in their lifetime. In certain shamanic cultures, it is tradition that all members of the tribe partake of the mushroom once a year. What I am saying is that – like Carlos Castaneda – my own mind was originally so deeply rooted in The Consensual World and its intrinsic programs that even after a lifetime of metaphysical pursuits, attempts at meditation and other methods of self-empowerment, I remained unable to make that quantum leap of perception which seems to be required to really begin to embrace the kind of understanding necessary to an evolution of consciousness.

I do know of people who have experienced that quantum leap without the use of forbidden fruit. I refuse to refer to psilocybin mushrooms as a drug anymore than I would refer to ginseng as a drug. Both are simply organic substances used to heal the body and mind long before modern medicine sprung into being. The word "drug", in this case, is merely part of the cultural program designed to scare the seeker away from the search. And yet, more than any other single external force, they cured me of my soul-sickness by enabling me to step outside the program and take a look around at the true nature of self, reality and eternity. Is it any wonder they are categorized as illegal by the powers that be?

Consider this: if a substance existed which had the potential to reveal the total truth of the world – including the phantom nature of governments and religions, the two most powerful institutions on the planet – does it not stand to reason that both those institutions would go to extreme lengths to keep that substance out of the hands of their subjects? One institution protects itself with The Law. The other re-draws the substance into the shape of an apple and touts it as the tool of the devil – "forbidden fruit", "forbidden knowledge". For someone even just beginning on this path, it shouldn't be difficult to figure out that there is something to hide. That something is indeed forbidden knowledge – the knowledge that has the power to topple governments and religions and empower Man to take control and responsibility for his own potential evolution. Of course, when and if Man begins to do that on a wide-spread basis, it stands to reason those very governments and religions will fall. And so, once again, the wizards of society are hiding behind their bureaucratic guises and inside their papal disguises, telling us to pay no attention to the man behind the curtain.

Take a closer look. What is it these institutions are trying to protect if not their own self-serving illusions of power and self-importance.

The bottom line is simply this: we use penicillin to cure the infections of the body, working in conjunction with the patient's own immune system. In certain cases, if used responsibly and with intent, psilocybin mushrooms and other shamanic substances can be used to cure the infections of the soul by giving us a glimpse of what we can be, a glimpse of the butterfly imprisoned inside the chrysalis.

Acting Lessons
Stalking Expectations and Belief Systems

"Act like a lady!" "Act like a warrior!" "Act like a **nagual**!"
Acting...

When I was a little girl and my mother told me to "act like a lady" in church, I wondered if that meant I would have to douse myself in cheap perfume, put on a flowered dress that stank of stale beer, wear blue eye shadow so thick it would crack, and give blow jobs to bald deacons in the dressing room of the choir loft - because that was my perception of how "ladies" acted in the church where I grew up.

When I asked her one day why she wanted me to "act like a lady", she began explaining the attributes of a lady. A lady walks with good posture and always smiles when meeting eyes with someone. A lady wears her best dress on Sunday, and never speaks to a gentleman unless he speaks first. A lady does not run through the cemetery with her friends after Sunday School, nor does a lady talk above the volume of a soft murmur. And above all else, a lady never asks questions - for to do so implies a masculine curiosity that is not becoming to a lady.

I was very young at the time these rules were laid down to me, and suffice it to say I found them bizarre and constrictive at best, and so I was never much of a lady. Secretly, I suspect my mother was proud of the fact that I was a tomboy with a penchant for bringing home stray cats, and for driving the preacher crazy with all my questions that couldn't be answered.

But there were those words, which she repeated nonetheless – not necessarily because she believed them, but because they were part of *her* role, *her* costume, *her* mask.

"Act like a lady." Act.

As I grew older, I understood what was intended by the words, but it didn't make the sentiment itself any less insane in my book. While my art teacher was fond of saying, "Think for yourself and paint what is in your heart's eye," my home economics teacher would spew forth such platitudes as, "Learn all you can in my class, girls, so you'll be able to attract a good man, and cook a decent meal for your husband and children." And, of course, this was often accompanied by the suggestion: "And don't forget to act like ladies around the boys!"

I often found myself wondering even as far back as early childhood why such an emphasis was placed on attempting to convince others that we were somehow different than we actually are. On the one hand, well-meaning teachers and parents would say, "Just be yourself." On the other hand, there was that war cry: "Act like a lady! Act like a winner! Act like a Christian! Act like an American!"

As I grew older and eventually embarked on this path, I began to realize just how disassociated most people really are from their own authenticity - largely because most of them spend their lives acting and pretending. But even more curious is the fact that there comes a point when the actors forget they are acting, and start to believe it is somehow real... and worse still, is when their own expectations begin to manifest in the very same words they may have shunned as children, and they start telling others to "Act like a lady!" Chances are, they don't even hear themselves, or if they do, they have simply bought into the program that was put onto them by their parents, and their parents before them. Ignorance is also a lineage, when one really examines it.

I can write a lot of that off to the predictable behavior of phantoms. Point is - when I am dealing with phantoms, it is a given that they will behave as phantoms and hold the values of phantoms and *act* like phantoms.

But when I am dealing with people who profess to be warriors, and I hear that type of program coming out of their mouth, I am amazed that they do not hear their own rhetoric. Recently, during an otherwise neutral conversation with a man I've known for years, he began saying to me, "Act like a nagual, Della! If you don't act like a nagual, then you're not one!"

So what does a nagual "act" like? Does she walk around all day spouting great wisdom and smacking others on the back in an attempt to shift their assemblage point? Does a nagual sit by a campfire in the desert eating ayahuasca and doling out peyote buttons to would-be apprentices?

What does a nagual _act_ like?

How does a brunette act? How does a man with green eyes act? How does a black man act? How does an Asian woman act?

Once we break free of our expectations and our self-imposed stereotypes, we will generally find that most people have at their core an authenticity which has nothing to do with *what* they are, but with *who* they are. The key to recognizing authenticity in others is learning to recognize it in ourselves - and that's one of the hardest tasks seekers face, for it involves the willingness to let go of belief systems and expectations which are directly and deeply related to one's own ego and need to feel they are right.

What needs to be recognized is that so much of what we *think we know* is really only what we have *come to believe* - and when we are willing to examine our own expectations and belief systems is when we have a prime opportunity to expand our awareness in multiple directions through a simple act of letting go of some _idea_ about someone else that has absolutely nothing to do with the person whatsoever. Not all naguals are going to live up to your expectations of don Juan, and not all blondes are dumb. Those are nothing more than stereotyped belief systems, and *only* when they are released does the warrior engage with the opportunity to really *see* what-is, instead of only *believing* in his own pre-existing notions of what something *should* be. If you spend your whole life looking for don Juan, you may miss out on the man or woman of knowledge who is sitting next to you on the bus because they don't live up to what you *think* they *should* be.

And then, of course, there are the secondary programs running in the background which support the primary program. For example, dontcha just love the logic when someone says, "If you *say* you are a teacher, then you aren't. If you *say* you are a nagual, you obviously aren't!"

Kinda like the old Monty Python logic of *Life of Brian*. Having been mistaken for Christ, Brian adamantly protests to a large crowd of followers, "I am *not* the messiah!" And, from deep in the crowd, a little voice says, "Only the true messiah denies his divinity!"

Can't win.

Maybe your authentic self isn't all sweetness and light - and if you *are* authentic, that is most likely the case. I am highly suspicious of anyone who is always laughing or smiling and has only nice things to say. That person, in all likelihood, is not being authentic with me - and, worse, they are not being authentic with themselves.

So is that to say authenticity allows us to mope around or hurl insults at passersby on the street because that is how we truly feel? Sure, you can do that, but as with all things, there are consequences to one's actions, so this is where the advanced seeker begins stalking herself with the art of **controlled folly**, working hand in hand with an increasing connection to silent knowing and the Other.

What we are doing is a *system* of knowledge, and so it is really only when all of the components of the system begin to work together in energetic compatibility that we realize the best results in our own unique journey.

It's one matter to be impeccable in all things, but even if one practices impeccability with ruthless intent, it may not be sufficient to lead the warrior to freedom if, for example, the warrior has not lost self-importance, or has not sufficiently released the energy hooks from her past (whether through recapitulation or through the art of becoming a **teflon warrior**). And even if a warrior has lost self-importance, but has not abandoned dependence on the egoic ramblings of her own internal dialog, the system is not functioning at full capacity, and will most likely fail at some point. We cannot embrace our totality if we are still clinging to false identities or erroneous belief systems, for the totality is what we find when we emerge from those dark shadows and into the luminosity of our own unique being.

Put another way - we cannot be whole for as long as we are the least bit invested in what others think of us, and so there comes a point in a warrior's life when s/he has some tough choices to make and, in addition, must come face to face with her own darkest fears and self-doubts.

Man is really a machine,
his primary function to be a grave digger
at his life-long funeral procession
of petty dramas and clichés.

Embracing the Dark Side
It's okay to be pissed off

May 3, 2005

There are some spiritual teachers who advocate what amounts to the suppression of emotion – or what was called by one man I once worked with, "going into observe mode" - so that even when a warrior may have every right and reason to be angry or joyous, the result would be essentially standing to the side, observing the situation from a more detached perspective, with a more placid acceptance of "what is". I put several phrases in quote marks because these have come to sound like buzz words – though I had not been able to adequately define why these buzz words were troublesome. Something about this whole idea of "observe mode" has never felt right on an intuitive level, and at long last I believe I may have stumbled onto a partial explanation.

Since I first embarked on this journey, I have encountered a lot of metaphysical teachers (from Toltec to Buddhist and everything in between) who attempt to teach their apprentices that our "negative" emotions are somehow tantamount to evil itself, and must therefore be excised, or at the very least controlled to the point that the apprentice automatically goes into "observe mode" at the first sign of any potential negative reaction. In other words, one reaction is simply substituted for another, a different program is brought into play, but it's still a program. I'm going to use anger as the emotion *du jour*, but any of the traditional "negative" emotions could be substituted.

There have been several discussions about this, and yet I still did not feel satisfied that I had really been able to isolate precisely why this idea of suppressing our emotions feels every bit as wrong to me as the idea of an extant deity on a golden throne answering to the name of God. And yet, every time I would hear a warrior say something to the effect of, "I was really pissed off that my husband kicked the dog, but I went into observe mode so as to remain detached," I would be left with a feeling that said, quite simply, *That ain't right.*

Finally, I had a personal epiphany which explains why these "observe mode" methods so highly touted by certain mystical teachers simply do not work in the big picture. In a sense, it's because teaching an apprentice to go into observe mode can end up being more like a bandaid over a gushing artery. It stems the flow for awhile, but doesn't fix the underlying problem. It's like teaching a child to say "darn" instead of "damn" - one may appear more acceptable, but the underlying problem still remains. All that has changed is how it is being expressed. Teachers who employ such methods may help an apprentice identify certain behaviors and even suggest ways to staunch the undesirable behavior, such as "going into observe mode" or "become transparent", but what I've really observed is that this can end up replacing one pre-programmed response with another - i.e., you're only substituting "observe mode" for "anger mode", but the anger is still present. There is no authenticity in this approach – just a temporary bypass of one false self for another false self.

Trying to behave like a Vulcan is only another role-playing game - it's simply not real because we're not really Vulcans. It's not in our nature. So what I've learned to do is to use my anger productively and ruthlessly - literally change the "molecular nature" of anger into creative godforce, for example. Rather like using a propane-fed fire to power a refrigerator in your camper. Using "negative" energy to create something positive, rather than trying to squelch or ignore the negative energy because we've been programmed to think that anything "negative" or "dark" is something to be eradicated, when the truth is that it is just another tool once we strip away the assignations and stigma put onto it by our own human belief systems.

In the big picture, until we leave this earth, we're still human and that's just the way it is. So where my method differs from that of many other teachers is that I don't try to teach people to be "peaceful warriors", but to use their emotions with awareness and ruthless impeccability.

In some of my online forums and on my website, I've often talked about the power howl. That's one way I channel anger into something more creative. In my "real job", I work special event festivals as a merchant, and so our business is outdoors, at the mercy of the elements; and in most cases, we camp outdoors and sleep under the stars, often falling asleep to the sounds of drumming and the clanging of zils at renaissance faires, or the wail of bagpipes at Scottish Highland Games. That's the cool part of it. But there's a darker side. This past weekend up at Shasta, it rained all night on Friday and showed no signs of stopping as of 9:45 a.m. The faire was scheduled to open at 10 a.m. I was furious - because we had driven 12 hours; I was directly across from my primary competitor; we had already had some rather serious damage to the business inventory due to the rain; my sleeping bag and my body were soaking wet; I'd had no sleep due to all of the above... and so I walked out behind the booth, facing the Sacramento River, and instead of going into some mode of "acceptance", I pointed my nose skyward, let the river's power flow through my veins, and howled like a demented banshee at the top of my lungs. (At a ren faire, this isn't seen as especially strange... luckily). As I howled, I had the thought - *I need to make enough money this weekend to publish my book!* (Not to mention, paying the usual household bills...)

It stopped raining precisely at 10 a.m. as the opening guns of the faire sounded. And while I didn't make quite enough money to publish the book outright, I did make enough for a hefty down payment. Believe what you will, but I am convinced that when I channeled my anger into *intent*, it was sufficient to alter the flow of reality because literally everyone else I know (other merchants, faire-goers and guild actors) had all basically said, "Que se'ra," with regard to the rain. Well, I don't que se'ra. I create reality, and I use every ounce of my humanness to do it – dark, light, negative, positive, anger, love… and everything in between. Had I simply gone into "observe mode", I would be observing someone else's reality instead of creating my own. Had I gone into observe mode, I wholly believe the rain would have continued through the weekend, as it was "supposta" do according to the weather report.

I could be wrong, of course. Maybe the rain would've stopped anyway – in which case, all those cheerful bliss-ninnies in their flowing white dresses would be justified in saying, "If you had simply observed, you would have saved your energy." Maybe. But who's to say? All I know is that whenever I have really had good cause to howl in earnest with intent, something quite miraculous often happens.

It's okay to be human. It's even okay to get pissed off – because that's part of being human. What matters for warriors is learning how to channel the energy of the "negative" emotions into the power of Intent. That, to me, is one definition of sorcery.

The door between realities
stands open a crack,
revealing the shadows still to come,
the effect of moonlight on tombstones.

Wings, Wind & Summer's End
No tomorrow, no yesterdays

September 1, 2004

Lit the candle lanterns in the cactus garden tonight and sat outside underneath the stars for a long time. The wind has turned soft, and though still warm with the breath of summer, the oppressive desert heat has finally begun to dissipate. Autumn peeks in at the corners of reality, still too far away to touch.

As I sat in my lawn chair with the weenie dogs bounding playfully inside the boundaries of the little picket fence, and the older dog crashed out on her side in the warm sand, there was a single moment when it seemed everything had simply stopped. There was no time. No tomorrow. No yesterdays. There was only that one single moment isolated like a single cell underneath a microscope, and a sense of Knowing this was how it would always be.

Impossible to explain, but it was like a single frame in a movie, preserved for all of eternity. The universe will eventually collapse back in on itself, then expand again, and if quantum theories have any accuracy whatsoever, everything that is in the now, will be again. And again. And again. The moment of stillness was almost like passing oneself in that corridor between expansion and collapse - as if the Self I am in the now, and the selves I have been in all those otherworlds were waving at one another across the abyss, eternal participants in some infinite dance of energy over which they have no control whatsoever. So there is nothing to do but laugh.

The universe seemed to have a secret. It hummed quietly to itself, and threw falling stars the way a flower girl tosses rose petals in the path of the bride. And yet, there was a melancholy, too, for what I was seeing was a dark wedding between the mortal self and the eternal Other - and though that is obviously the goal of the sorcerer/seeker, there is nonetheless a sadness in recognizing that this mortal coil is finite, gathered up out of the dust, and to the dust destined to return.

On one level, I understand that and accept it as the transmigration of the soul from the mortal coil into the eternal energy-double. And yet, there is a tiny voice inside me that continues to cry out, "Why? Why is it like this, when it could be like _that_ instead? Why do we travel the universe in these fragile human bodies when we could just as easily be made of photons of light or subatomic particles of dark matter? Why is it the ultimate irony that life is so beautiful, when it is seemingly destined by our organic nature to end in death?"

Water gurgling in the little pond-fountain sputtered, caught in a toss of wind.

"This is the path of the Spirit," the voice of gnosis tells me with an utter sense of peace and acceptance. "The cocoon knows only that it is a cocoon, and wants only to go on being a cocoon. Only after it spreads its wings does it realize that the whole point of the journey is learning to fly."

Upon leaving the garden to return to the house, I left a single candle burning in the archway that leads from here to there, from the known and into the unknown.

So I go on, learning to fly, feeling at times all too heavy. My wings are made of starsilk and winter-wind, candle breath and moon veins.

I am only a symbol
and a shadow
of what I truly Am

A Matter of Perspective

August, 2006

There's a story I often tell when working with newbie warriors who are processing through guilt of some sort.

What determines a hero or a villain is nothing more than random chance. Let's say a friend tells you he's going to jump off a cliff because his wife just left him, he has terminal cancer, and the bank has begun foreclosure procedures on his house because he can't pay his bills. The two of you are standing at the edge of the abyss, and he starts to jump, but because you love him, you reach out and pull him back to safety.

Okay... that's the scenario.

Now, let's say that after you pull him back from the abyss, his wife has a change of heart and decides to stay with him. He falls in love with her all over again, and that sends the cancer into spontaneous remission. Because he's now able to work again, the bank gives him an extension, and he is able to pay his bills and get his life back in order. You're a hero - because if you hadn't pulled him back from the cliff, he'd be deader'n a doornail.

Or...

Let's say you pull him back from the cliff, but his wife *doesn't* change her mind. She leaves him, and his disease gets worse instead of better. He lapses into a long-term coma, the house is repossessed by the bank, and so there's not only no inheritance for his children, but his remaining family is left with his medical bills, and must take out liens on their own property in an attempt to do what's "right", and as a result of all of this, even *more* lives are ruined. You're a schmuck! You shouldda let him jump!

And yet... the action you took was precisely the same, and can only be judged in hindsight by the outcome. *The. Action. Was. Precisely. The. Same.*

Half Past Shadows
Recapitulating Parallel Lines

Traffic was moving at a steady pace; I was in the fast lane leading the pack; and so it made little sense when I found myself cutting across 5 lanes of freeway to dive onto the off ramp leading to The Past. The road to Ixtlan[2], the trail that goes toward a destination which exists in memory, the path of shadows skirting the edges of recapitulations long finished. The road to where I was living at the time I first met Orlando in manifestation.

The hillsides which had once bloomed vibrant yellow with so many wildflowers were now covered with a different kind of transplant - the urban virus which continues to spread like an out-of-control cancer on the face of the land, houses so close together the rooftops must certainly rub paint in a strong wind, with yards barely big enough for a single bush and a small dog to pee on it. Not the way man was meant to live, certainly, but this is no longer the world in which I grew up, so I have come to accept that in all likelihood, this is no longer the same species of human, either.

Heat pressed against the window of the Suburban as I looked around, catching brief glimpses of some past self darting here and there in a car I once owned. The karate studio is still where I left it, but expanded into 3 suites now. The real estate office where I used to work has become a chic health food boutique, and the house where I used to live has been stripped bare of its vegetation to make room for a cement driveway.

It occurs to me that I am not particularly interested in my own past. Instead, I am headed toward the location where I first met Orlando and where I last had contact with him. For a moment, as I glance out across the hillsides which are too

---

[2] A reference to Carlos Castaneda's "Journey to Ixtlan".

steep to build upon, I see a ghostly figure of a young woman riding a pale horse through the vast expanse of tall green wild grass. But when I look again, it is only a mirage, though the voice of gnosis whispers, unbidden, "She's still out there somewhere." Perhaps she is. That phantom self of my phantom past - always searching for something alone in those hills at dusk, never satisfied, always restless.

Several years ago, shortly after embarking on this journey, I had reason to pass through this shadow past again - and as I drove through the same area in perhaps 1995, that same voice of gnosis had informed me, "You are no longer the same girl who once rode her horse through these hills." We move on, but we leave tracings behind, images painted on the surface of water, shimmering in the hologram of our personal history. Sometimes, if we are sorcerers, we may be able to reach out and touch them, guide them, or at least whisper in their ear from the future past.

As I approach the corner where Orlando's house once stood, I wonder what I will find now that time has moved on past those crazy and inexplicable events frozen in memory. Though I have known for several years that the house itself had been torn down, it had been rumored that the city intended to build offices on the land. But instead there is only a vacant lot which has been transformed into a small park - actually an extension of a much larger park across the street. Decorative black gravel covers all traces of where the foundation once lay, and all that remains of the original landscaping are two California pepper trees - which have grown far taller and stronger than the last time I saw them. What I immediately notice is that each of the trees has four primary trunks, and for a split second, it's as if I am looking at two double beings, standing side by side. A chill passes through my body, and a vision whispers delicately across the mind's eye. Each tree is a nagual, one on either side of the black gravel path. And though each is whole unto itself, there is strength in their unity, each lending shade to the other's roots, roots themselves entangling in an eternal embrace of the earth, stretching deeper and deeper into the black soil of the unknown, searching for sustenance.

For a moment, I stop the car and just sit there at the edge of the park, looking into a past that is far behind, and yet ever-present in the hologram of the Now. The voice of gnosis asks, "What are the trees telling you?"

Impossible to say, really. The layers of meaning stretch decades into my personal yesterdays, and may have relevance only to myself. And yet, there was something there I needed to see. It would be easy enough to say the trees are Orlando and myself, yet it was more than that. Each was whole unto itself, yet each had four trunks - rather like the four compartments of a nagual's energy body as it appears to a Seer.

Traffic streamed by on a road that was barely traveled when I lived in the area, and for a split second, I was transported 3,000 miles distant, back to the property where I myself grew up in central Florida. I was able to visit that old place about 2 years before, and could barely recognize where I had spent the first 17 years of my life. The land had been reclaimed by nature - creeping vines and a sinkhole that had filled with water to make the land unusable. I had made the same observation before - that both my old stomping ground and Orlando's had come to be vacant spaces in the middle of otherwise thriving cities, but somehow today that realization struck me with renewed strength. A sense of synchronicity that was eerie in its intensity settled around me.

The voice of gnosis murmured through the crack between the worlds, "There are parallel lines that cross at infinity." Sometimes we get a preview.

Before I drove away, I watched the heat monkeys dancing on the black gravel path, energy in motion that swirled and wriggled on the canvas of the hologram, uncatachable, but not invisible. And for a single moment, I was looking into the otherworld where past and future collide, where the little white house is still standing at the edge of the infinite, with its front door open and its cracked front step adorned with fallen leaves and tiny puddles of rain.

There are parallel lines that cross at infinity. Knowing this, the double leaves the door ajar and beckons us to find our way home.

Later on, back home after a long excursion, I was standing in the kitchen thinking about the events of the morning, the observations, and what it might all mean. I became aware of a presence at my back. Familiar, warm, but with an edge of danger, it leaned close and there was a sensation of arms being wrapped around me from behind, just a hint of breath against my shoulder. It occurred to me to panic, wondering briefly if someone had broken into the house.

So I just stood there, took a cautious breath, and waited.

"There are parallel *lives* that cross at infinity," Orlando whispered with no small amount of amusement.

Oh. Now I see.

In fact... opens up a whole other world of worlds.

Common Sense & Carousel Horses
Seasons of Change

October 24, 2005

The hand of night has chosen a blacker shade of black gloves, and the October carnival has come to town, though there are no grinning carnies, no cotton candy and no half-eaten corn dogs dropped on the ground.

As our season winds down and we are greeted by almost two months of down time, I find myself in the midst of an odd melancholy which appears to have no rational origins. The world of illusions has become even more illusory, if possible, and the "carnival" might be described as a merry-go-round of souls going through the motions of a life, enacting little scenes here and there, hopping on and off of painted horses or broken-down chariots, laughing and crying equally, spinning through a colorful miasma of costumes and skits, understanding neither the script nor the stage on which it is played out like some wobbly high school production of *Carousel* being directed by a madman, and choreographed by two poodles holding flashlights in their teeth.

It makes no sense, but even if it did, even *that* would only be an agreement within the agreement, while warriors stand to the side watching it all unfold like the petals of a flower destined to wilt and eventually drop, unnoticed, into the abyss. What is "sense"? I found myself asking that question this past weekend when someone wondered aloud why no one seems to have common sense any longer. That was when I first heard the words fall from my lips, "Common sense is no longer common."

So I asked myself - is common sense really what is meant by "the right way to live"? Sometimes I think so. Other times, even that is only a painted eye on a carousel horse somewhere in the madhouse of a world that is nothing at all like we have been taught to believe. If there is a downside to discovering our authentic self, it may be summed up with the realization that we are no longer the least bit interested in acting out our roles, playing our parts, or participating in the design of props. I could say "I want to direct!" but even that isn't true.

It may also be expressed in a single grunt. "Hunh!" The sound one makes when realizing – abruptly – that this is all there is. That's how the magic trick works. The man behind the curtain is just a man.

Perhaps part of my current mood stems from the fact that I find myself somewhat unsettled for the first time in awhile - another sign and symptom of something Orlando has been warning about for almost a year now. What he has referred to as "a season of change". Ominous words - particularly to someone who will readily admit that she does not always welcome such "change" with open arms.

As described in the introduction, there came a time - a day I never really believed would come - when Orlando said to me, "I have given you all the pieces of the puzzle. There is no more I can teach you at this time." At first, I must admit I didn't even believe it when it happened. This path does seem to go through stages - not unlike the spinning horses in that madhouse carnival, only with perhaps slightly more purpose (if "purpose" may even be perceived to exist outside of the agreement). It was shortly after Orlando gave me that message that he began pointing me in the direction of my own assimilation - which has been an ongoing process for the past 5 years, and has included such tools as the creation of my website, various forums, my online journals, and the writing of my first book, *Quantum Shaman: Diary of a Nagual Woman.*

Now, oddly enough, I find myself at a position not unlike Orlando described when pressed about saying he had no more to teach us. What I am discovering is that I have little to say that hasn't already been said at least a thousand times, and in looking back over what has been written on my forums, in my journals, and on my website over the past 5 years, I'm also inclined to say... "I've revealed all the pieces of the puzzle I possess."

October is a fierce teacher and a demanding lover, to be sure. Having unveiled and assimilated the authentic self... one can only look at the road outside the window and accept that it leads everywhere or nowhere, depending entirely on the choices we make. Left, right, full speed ahead or standing still. Where are the carousel horses running to?

Fever Dreaming
The view from inside the egg

January 9, 2005

Rain scratches at the window above my head, and the room has transformed to a purple egg in which I toss and turn, halfway between sleep and waking, a feverish traveler through the crack between the worlds. Time is nothing more than a line drawn in the sand. Free will enables me to step over it, beyond it, or erase the line altogether.

I sit up to see that this bedroom is not what I thought it was in waking life. An endless array of halls lead in and out, some well lit, others dark. I touch the sides of the egg and it becomes illuminated - pulsing, producing a soft humming sound like a slow, electronic heartbeat.

For a century or two, I drift in and out of otherworlds. "Tortoiseshell sunglasses are coming back in style," I'm told, though the message seems to have little significance and only makes me smile, even though I am shown a factory in China where thousands of workers are assembling next year's manufactured fad. *It's all illusion*, I whisper. But no one hears.

Back inside the egg, I find myself fascinated with the long corridors coming into the room - entrances and exits I cannot recall ever having seen before. In one of them - a corridor in half-light, dusk-light, twilight – Orlando emerges in a fine Armani tux, carrying a black wedding cake, which he holds out to me in offering.

For a moment, I can only be amused, sitting there in inside the shell of my delirium with my legs curled under me, foolishly feeling safe despite the fact that my Other is standing in front of me, dressed to kill and bearing a gift symbolic of so many things he has said in the past.

> *Let me court you and let it be slow and easy. My caresses will come, and my kiss will follow, but I am as hungry for the long slow dance of Life itself as you are hungry to be in my*

58

arms. This is how we feed one another, bride and groom,
symbiots at our rehearsal banquet. Our wedding cake will
be black, for that is the color of creation from which all things
become manifest. I will feed it to you from my heart.

Words written nearly a decade ago come back to me
as clearly as if just having read them, and some little voice
from outside the egg whispers, "Time is an illusion, too.
You are already dead and forever alive. The immortals are
laughing at Schroedinger's cat."

In some other world seemingly disconnected by a
thousand light-years, I hear a sound which I recognize as my
own labored breathing, and at the same time I am *seeing* how
fragile it is. Between one breath and the next, eternity waits.

"I want to grow old on some serene front porch with
Wendy at my side, an old dog at my feet and a couple of
calico cats in my lap," I hear myself say.

Orlando smiles mischievously, dipping one finger into the
thick black icing, touching it to the tip of his tongue. Might as
well be the serpent and the apple.

"Life is but a dream," he tells me with tenderness and
affection. "When it is time to awaken, the egg will dissolve."

And then it was night for a long, long time.

She washes broken windows
in a house of ruins
haunted by restless spirits.
A rice bowl sits untouched
on pink formica countertop,
just another prop
in a life of linear mirages.

Jammin' On the Magic
What's that gonna look like?

December 10, 2007

> *"My function is very different from the function of Gautama Buddha. His function is only a small part of my philosophy. I want individuals to become enlightened, but I want also the whole of humanity to rise with the enlightened people. They may not become enlightened, but at least become conscious enough so that nations disappear, religions disappear, races disappear, and we can live as one humanity, as one earth." - Osho*

It's a nice idea.

But I'm not sure enlightenment or expanded awareness can occur by osmosis. At that point, it would seem to me like a paradigm shift. But without the deeper levels of understanding that come from doing the work, such shifts are destined to fail, which results in the lowering of the lowest common denominator.

I realize this isn't a particularly popular view, but I'm much more inclined to think it really is a matter of survival of the fittest, and that we are dealing with at least two different species of humans on the planet right now. As to which will emerge victorious? Who's to say - but probably neither, in the big picture.

The struggle for enlightenment has always been purely an individual effort, and I see no evidence that it will ever be otherwise.

A group of people once met here at my house for what amounted to a spiritual jam session - some of the most progressive thinkers in this area just sitting around on the front porch, a few drums, a couple of joints... and this one fellow who was highly esteemed by the locals kept talking about how, "We're gonna jam on the magic, I tell you! We're gonna swim with the dolphins and walk with our toes in the sand, and we're gonna jam on the magic until the whole world sings with us and we're all just One with Gaia!"

Well, when I asked him, "Daniel, could you give me a better idea of how this 'jamming on the magic' is going to look?" all conversation stopped for a moment. All eyes turned to me. It was as if I had suddenly tripped over the elephant in the room, and in doing so, forced an awareness that was unwelcome.

Daniel composed himself and launched into a diatribe about how, "We're just going to pour the energy into the magic, Della! Don't you get it? And when other people see how it's working, they'll want to be part of it, and it's like a contagion of good vibes and magic!"

Being a curmudgeon of sorts, this did not satisfy me. "Okay, I hear what you're saying, but I'm asking you how it is going to look. How is it going to work at the level of energy, at the level of Do-ing." I didn't have the heart to tell him there aren't any dolphins in the desert.

By the end of the evening, Daniel had declared to the group that I was just "stepping on the magic." Ah well... Maybe that was true to a minor extent, but the bottom line is that if we cannot visualize *how* something is going to work, chances are it is only a nice fantasy that will never have the power to take off. I've heard too many well-meaning gurus trying to sell us on their vision of a utopian society - so while Osho may have a good vision, I'd need to ask him, "And how is that going to work? How is it going to look? And how are you going to implement it in the real world?"

When the Wright Brothers thought of flying, they didn't just sit on somebody's front porch and talk about "jamming on the magic." They went out, learned about aerodynamics, and actually built a working model out of the raw stuff of their visions.

When I personally set out to do work on the spiritual path, I have to be able to see some semblance of how it looks, and how it works. That's why I refer to my work as "quantum shamanism™." If it isn't quantifiable - at least in concept - chances are the dream is going to fall into one of those gaps which is usually expressed by, "And then... somehow... the contraption lifts off the ground and flies."

Better define "somehow" before you get in the cockpit.

First shaman created First Man and First Woman with a thought. Secretly, he is both of those beings, split in two so he will not be alone in the world. I understand this because I-Am this.

Karma
Wishful thinking?

January, 2006

The whole idea of karma has never rung true with me - largely because it is too easy, and secondly because it implies some sense of fairness within the universe which I have never observed. There is balance (impeccable balance, actually), but fairness? Nada. That's why, when I hear someone say of a murderer or a child molester, "Oh, his karma will catch up to him," my instant reaction is more likely a sad sigh rather than any nod of agreement - even though it would make me feel better to think karma is alive and well.

Because there is no fairness, my feeling with regard to cruelty is that it is always an entirely human choice. In the animal kingdom, even when dealing with predator/prey situations which might be grisly or violent, I don't sense any cruelty from it. The coyote doesn't hunt for sport. The serpent doesn't torture the mouse. The peregrine doesn't dull her talons to make the rat suffer before it dies. The mountain lion doesn't hunt the jackrabbit to extinction just to feel the power of killing. Only humans seem to torture one another and run rampant through their environment to the point that they begin to threaten even their own survival.

As a result, I can only surmise that humans are completely out of balance - not only out of balance with nature, but within themselves. Don Juan might say they have lost touch with "the right way to live", and so they have lost any sense of empathy. They have forgotten how to look out through the eyes of the other creatures on this planet, and so their world is narrow, limited, and altogether unjust.

As an example, our fascination with the act of war has perpetuated and exacerbated our sense of cruelty. I recently went to see the movie, *Master and Commander*, and though I found it to be an excellent film overall, I kept thinking to myself that if I had a wide open sea in front of me, I really couldn't be bothered to wage someone else's war, when it was already patently obvious that to do so was going to result in the death, dismemberment, pain and suffering of all those in my care - best friends, extended family, children. But for the sake of squabbling over some imagined line in the sand, or trying to enforce an agreement (you *will* believe as I believe or I will kill you), humans seem quite willing to pump lead into one another's bodies, ram steel swords into one another's chests, drop bombs onto foreign cities, and generally engage in acts of cruelty beyond all imagining.

We are at the top of the food chain (for now), and yet in so many ways, we are far less evolved than our counterparts in the animal kingdom. There are legends in many shamanic cultures which say that when we developed language, we lost all ability to communicate. We traded words for empathy, entertainment for experience.

As warriors, we strive to have awareness within ourselves - empathy with others of our own kind, and others *not* of our kind. Whenever I look at someone (human or animal) and remind myself that this is a living being who feels fear and love and pain, a living being who is just struggling to survive and get through its day... then it becomes possible to walk a mile in the other man's moccasins. What hurts you will hurt him... and then cruelty becomes a thing of the past.

Yes, it really *is* that simple.

Solstice Recapitulation
Re-evaluating the search for the authentic self

December 21, 2008

Over the years of the journey, we've talked about enlightenment, the matrix, Plato's cave, transmogrification, vampires, empires, con jobs, snow jobs, blow jobs, and the meaning of life. At times, I find myself asking... Where are we going with this? What do we hope to accomplish here? Even if we were all to come to a single agreement - God is a giant potato and we will all be freedom fries in the afterlife which is promised to us by The Great Spud - so what? *Really*. So what? Where does the agreement get us? What does it do for us? Does it advance us, or does it actually limit us? Are we here seeking freedom, or just arguing for our limitations?

When I initially opened my first discussion group - "The Quantum Forum" - it was largely for my own assimilation, a place to bounce my ideas off of others on a similar journey, challenge my beliefs to the core through direct interaction with other warriors who were wrestling with the same concepts, and essentially form a foundation of my own Knowledge. Not for any great purpose. Just to see if I know, even remotely, who I am.

What I found was that the foundation not only held - though it went through several modifications and structural changes, which I see as an ongoing evolution - but it gave me a far deeper understanding of the workings of life than I ever would have believed possible. Understanding the double led to a much broader understanding of how consciousness functions, and with that understanding, I was able to formulate what amounts to a personal plan for burning with the fire from within, slipping past the eagle, and all those other tired old clichés which have run the high risk of becoming just words due to overexposure. But no matter. We all know what we're talking about:

**Experience>Assimilation>Knowledge>New
Experience>Deeper Assimilation>Evolving Knowledge.**

And so the cycle goes. And all plans are subject to last minute revisions.

Lately, however, I've found myself facing some serious dilemmas (giving credence to the notion that the path gets more difficult as we go along). I get about 20 emails per day on an average, most coming through the *Quantum Shaman*™ website. While most are simple in the sense that they may be someone just looking for a word of encouragement, there are some that are of a far more serious nature. Over the past month, I've gotten emails from one person who is at the brink of despair with health issues; another from a young man who has lost everything - home, family, career - and wants to know how he may apply his path to regaining his balance; another from someone having what she herself described as "a crisis of faith"; another from someone wanting to come live at my house and be my "apprentice"; and dozens more from people with issues that may appear far less serious to me, but are obviously every bit as serious to them.

Aside from ascertaining that these folks had exhausted all normal channels first (doctors, psychologists, or what-have-you), I used to ask myself what I could do to help these people. Now, I just write to them and hope that Spirit will open whatever connection is required so that my words might point them in the direction of whatever tool or understanding they are seeking. I never know, of course. All I can do is share my knowledge, share whatever tools I've found, and make sure the person I'm talking to knows that whatever path they are on is *their* path. "Here - take these tools, do what you Will with them - just don't try to recreate my path (or anyone else's) because then all you're doing is building sets on the stage of the play." Frustrating thing is, even when I have said to some of them, "I can't help you - I don't have the knowledge you're looking for," many will come back with something along the lines of, "Then help me to get to the place where you *can* help me. Do I need to take a workshop? Do I need to read any particular books, attend any particular seminars?"

No. No. And no.

Sure, I have workshops available on my website. They may even be helpful in overcoming some programs, or gaining some new techniques for stalking oneself, but ultimately no workshop or seminar is going to instill in anybody any real Knowledge. These are just tools. Take all the workshops you like. Go to all the seminars you want. But at the end of the day, if it doesn't *assimilate* into your life - if it isn't who *you* are - then it's all just finger-painting on the deck of *Titanic* while the boat is going down fast. Amusement. Entertainment. A do-ing that cannot substitute for simply *Being* present in one's life from moment to moment - aware, awake, filled with the love of being alive.

"So how do I wake myself up?" many ask. "How do I stay awake? How can I do with *my* double what you've done with yours?"

Maybe you can't. That's *my* journey. Maybe it isn't your destiny at all. If it were, I suspect you'd be do-ing it - manifesting it, creating it, experiencing it - instead of *looking* for it. So all I can say in that regard is the same thing that's been oft-repeated over the years. There is no path to *follow*. All you really need to do is ask yourself one question: What does your heart want to do? I'm not talking about the frilly emotional baggage that often gets associated with the phrase "path of heart". I'm talking about the nitty-gritty confrontation one does in one's own mirror. Do you want to be a stock broker or do you want to be a rock star? If you *do* want to be a rock star - now here's where it gets tricky - do you have the ability, the commitment, and a sufficient presence of Will to actually bring this into being?

Ain't easy.

So what does that mean in the big picture? If our heart wants to be a rock star, but we have a voice like Alvin the

Chipmunk, what to do? How do we apply the path of heart to our day to day lives? Do we work as a stock broker in the day and sing karaoke in the local pub at night? Maybe. If that's what satisfies your heart, then why not?

I always wanted to be a writer. Never was able to make a reasonable living at it for many reasons, but because it is the path of my heart, I write anyway. Too much for some to handle, I'm told. I started writing when I was about 11, on an old Royal typewriter that would cut your fingers to the bone if they slipped between the keys and down into the inner gazurkis. And in so many ways, *that* is how I created my double. *That* is how I summoned my own muse, and breathed him into being over the years. I don't expect anyone to understand that - and I certainly don't expect anyone to try to do it in the same way. Wouldn't work anyway, because it would be a recreation of someone else's path, rather than a crying out of the human heart into the void. If you want to meet your double - if that is truly the path of your heart - then you will Do what it takes to manifest that reality. For me, it was *Star Trek* and sci-fi and going out into the night and shaking my fist at the sky, saying to the empty place in my spirit, "If I can't come to you, I'll bring you to me!"

Shake your fist at the sky. Howl and dance. Do whatever it takes to manifest your dream, but for the love of life, don't try to manifest someone else's! How can you inhabit your authentic self if you're trying to be someone else? Buddha didn't hold the patent on awakening. It's been going on for thousands of years and has taken as many forms. And I dare say that those who *do* awaken will do it on their own terms, and not at the hands of any extant guru, yogi, swami, holy man or the like. Sure, those folk have some great tools to offer, but there comes that critical point when you have to hear the beat of *your* heart and no one else's. Then, and only then, will you have the ability to *be* the journey, instead of seeing yourself as some being *on* a journey.

At least several times a month, I have someone say they want to "walk the magical path" - but ultimately I have found that really isn't so. What they usually want is to sit at the gates and peer in at whatever magical kingdom they *believe* they want, but most simply are not willing to take even the first step toward manifesting the desires of their own heart. Why? Many reasons. Too many to list, but just to name the most prominent, I would say the foreign installation itself stops them at the threshold just by saying to them, "That's crazy! It's okay to dream it, but if you ever try to _be_ it, they'll lock you up & throw away the key!" (A lesson Dr. Frankenfurter learned the hard way).

Fear, in other words. Fear of losing one's sanity. Fear of a permanent displacement of the assemblage point. Fear of loneliness. Whatever it is... it is fear. The internal dialog. The consensus reality. The agreement. All of it. The checks and balances that hold us in stasis unless and until we simply decide to wake up.

And here's the thing. For those people who *do* only want to sit at the gates... That's okay. But if you truly want to live in the sorcerer's world - you *will*. Nothing and no one will be able to stop you, for *that* is the path of your heart. That is where your world will come alive and fill every aspect of your life - no longer any division between your spirituality and your real life persona. They will become one and the same – the assemblage point of the authentic self - or that hollow, empty place will remain and you will continue to be just an actor in your own drama. And that, too, is okay... if it's what you choose.

But _if_ you want to find that wholeness, that awakening into the sorcerer's world, you will risk everything. Maybe you will even lose everything. When I first started this journey, Orlando warned that it would cost me my friends, my family, and any sense of belonging to the so-called real world, and that has certainly turned out to be the case. Not because he said it would be so, but because that is where the journey has led over many years of experience and, at times, exhaustive effort on my part to prove him wrong! But, in the end, it is what it is.

Eyebrows raise, perhaps. "Is Della saying we should leave our families and join a cult?"

No. No. And no. If you think that, you need to clean out your ears.

What I *am* saying is that I have not found it possible (nor desirable) to attempt to maintain the polite facades required for "a normal life" - and that includes interaction with those who have tried to say to me over the years, "Can't you just be more positive? Can't you just be my friend and, by the way, here's the script for what I want you to say on any given occasion. Can't you just nod politely and pretend you agree with me? Can't you just be one of the guys? Can't you be this way or that way? Can't you be who *we* want you to be instead of who you are?"

No.

That's the price. And for most, it is too high. "Well, I want freedom, but if it means having to give up my family and friends, then I have to find some other way." Good - do so. Find another way! When Orlando said this journey would cost me everything, what he meant was that it would become a *choice* for me - because, ultimately, the journey itself holds far more value to me than family gatherings and polite dinners with old friends to discuss who's fucking whom and the proper care and feeding of rug rats. Don't get me wrong - those things are of ultimate value to some. Maybe to most. I just keep finding too many "Agent Smiths" taking on the mantra of the consensus reality, striving as always to drag us back into the programs. Phantoms on the road to Ixtlan, we call them in Toltec terms. Rest assured - they are very real, and the lure is a phenomenal force. A sense of belonging. Even love. "Just let go of all of this silly stuff you write about, Della, and you can be one of us. We'll love you and warm you and give you milk & cookies before you go to bed, and we'll all be together like a big, happy family."

Anybody here ever seen a happy family? I haven't. Oh, I've seen a lot of pageants and pretenses, but in my neck of the woods, most families aren't really happy nearly as much as they are stuck with one another by default. But no matter. That's *my* experience. It doesn't have to be yours.

I've had a strange and wonderful life. Hope it continues for a long, long time to come. Over the years, I've had some friends who have gazed in at my strange life, and wanted to be a part of it in some deeper way (whatever that means). They want to have the experiences I've had. Or they want me to produce Orlando for their amusement. Or they want to be along for the ride when I side-step this reality and enter a world where time goes missing and inorganic beings hold tea parties at the edge of the abyss. Yes, I've done these things. And yet... so what? They are, quite simply, *my* experiences. Yes, I believe others can have similar happenings, but those experiences have to be the ones *you* create - not anything that has been created for you in books, or tales by the fires of eternity. Your experiences. Yours alone.

And, yes, I will tell you that the price is high.

And yet...

If it is who you are, there is no price at all. You will follow your heart even if it leads you into hell, because what you will find is that you are perhaps happiest when battling the forces of hell, rather than sitting around the fire toasting marshmallows with all your personal demons.

Find *your* voice. Even if you sing like Alvin, it will be *your* song. Maybe nobody will love you for it. Maybe nobody will hate you for it. Doesn't matter. It's still your song, and there is not another one like it in all the universe.

Be the journey.

End of the Road
I found myself, but I don't know what to do with him!

October, 2008

I recently had a warrior say to me: "I have gone far down this path till there is no path." The sad truth about paths is that they do end, and there's nothing you can do about it from that point forward except to forge your own path. When I talk about the path it is seen on many different levels. There is what might be called a process in the beginning - some warriors connect with it through Toltec, others through Zen, others through various manifestations of shamanism. But there comes a time when one runs out of road, and there is just the warrior and the worlds, with no real path left to follow. You have the Knowledge, but no clear indicator of where to take it, what to do with it, nothing at all. Just you and the end of the road – and yet, it seems that when we run out of road is when the journey really begins. That's the part of the equation that is difficult, scary, and has caused more warriors to turn back than any encounter with allies or power plants.

When I think of the four enemies of a man of Knowledge (fear, clarity, power and old age/death), the way I see it is this: fear is obvious, and something we deal with as an ongoing enemy. Clarity comes and we revel in it - sometimes getting lost in it for years. But as we come to the end of the path, clarity shows us that there is no more process - just a vast, untouched universe waiting for the creator's hand. It's knowing that we _are_ the creator that gives us pause and brings us face to face with Power. Usually, there is a relatively long period of time during which we simply don't know what to do with our Power, and it's at that point that a lot of warriors turn back - *because they have become accustomed to being followers of a path rather than _forgers_ of a path.* When we're following that initial path (whether Toltec, Zen, Buddhism or whatever), if we are impeccable, it could be said we're not really following, but learning from the paths of others. But then comes that day when we have learned all our teachers can teach us, and we then have to go out and push the envelope of Knowledge "where no man has gone before." There's something to that old *Star Trek* cliché - because that is the warrior's ultimate journey. Where <u>no</u> man has gone before. You are the first, and so the "path" disappears from beneath your feet, leaving you only with whatever knowledge you have gleaned from your experiences.

A few years back, I was playing with a concept which I called "beyond human comprehension"; and a related concept "beyond human experience." This is the territory of the Infinite, which defies words almost entirely. But what it amounts to is that there is an almost physical pain/confusion/anguish which the warrior begins to experience when she comes up against this idea of "beyond human experience." There is much humans *cannot* comprehend, yet it is in the attempt to do so that we push the envelope beyond human experience. That pushing is, in itself, part of our evolution, part of the manner in which we peck at the egg from the inside in an attempt to see what we've always believed lies beyond our ability to experience. Where are the preceptors for this? Impossible to say until we experience it, which becomes the process of evolution.

Sadly, very few ever make it to the end of the path, because the sorcerer's secret is that the path itself is part of the ordinary world, and is comforting and alluring in so very many ways. To admit that the path *has* an end, and to find oneself facing only the vast Unknown means evolving to a new level of thinking, a new level of responsibility, a new level of awareness - and that is far scarier than anything on the path the warrior has taken to get to this point.

Be Careful What You Wish For
Do we foresee it or do we create it?

Stardate Unknown

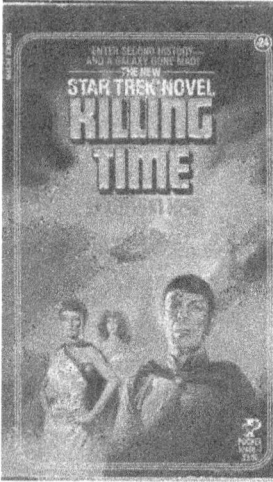

I've always wondered about a few things in my life that have no explanation – or, more precisely, two widely opposing possibilities. Do we foresee the future, or do we create it? In 1980, I wanted to take some time off to write my first book, *Killing Time* (a *Star Trek* novel), but the only way I could do it was to fabricate some phenomenal lie to impress my petty tyrant of a boss. So I told him I had to go back to Florida for a couple of weeks because my mother was going to have heart surgery. The woman had been healthy as a horse all her life, I had spoken with her on the phone not long before, and all was well. My boss was properly concerned, gave me a three week leave of absence, and so I sat down at my computer to begin weaving the tale of Kirk and Spock having to deal with a bunch of Romulans tampering with time (yes, they really *did* make the new *Star Trek* movie largely from my book, and no I never saw a dime, but that's another story for another day).

I was just getting to the relevant conundrum somewhere in the second chapter when the phone rang. My mother had been admitted to the hospital and was scheduled for triple bypass surgery the following morning. There was considerable doubt whether she would even survive the surgery, so I had to hop on a plane and actually *go* to Florida, almost like a character in a novel being told what to do by some invisible writer. (I hope Kirk and Spock don't *really* have to endure every ill cooked up for them by the scriptwriters, because my experience really *did* have all the earmarks of a script and I was just one of the players on the invisible stage.)

I tried to tell myself it was all just a very peculiar coincidence. I certainly didn't want to be responsible for me poor ol' mum's heart attack, after all, so inevitably the question came up... did I foresee it or did I cause it? (Jury's still out, by the way).

This preceded another strange happening that occurred in the vicinity of 1981. I was living in San Diego at the time, and a good friend had just moved into the area, a young woman who has also had strange experiences all her life, and has since embarked on a deeply committed spirit quest of her own. My own life at that time was odd, to say the least, in that I had been pursued by weird happenings all my life, but had not yet been able to figure them out. I was in my mid-20s, and to be blunt, I had been literally chased, pursued and at times terrified by a series of ongoing "manifestations". This often took the form of being stalked by a blue Camaro. This is a long story unto itself, but suffice it to say I had already confirmed that this was not an ordinary stalking. If they wanted to catch me, they could have – many times. If they wanted to kill me, they could have – many times. There was no real rhyme or reason to their behaviour – almost what one might expect from **tulpas** who were given a transient agenda, but without any real sense of purpose or direction. Put another way: it made no sense.

Diane and I had taken the late afternoon to walk down to a park at the edge of a canyon known locally as "the gorge" because it was so deep and lush in comparison to most of the desert landscape of San Diego. The park itself was on a cul-de-sac, about a block from my house, with the only access being across a narrow footbridge barely wide enough for a golf cart. The sun was just going below the horizon, but it was still full daylight, when all of a sudden I heard myself saying to Diane, "If a blue Camaro comes around that corner, we're going thataway!" I jerked my finger to the south, where several telephone poles had been rolled in a line to form a perimeter of the park - to keep cars from coming onto the grass.

There was no reason whatsoever for me to say this, for I had never been pursued by this anomaly when in the presence of any other human being. It was one of those things that always happened when I was alone, leading to accusations such as, "You're imagining it." "Obviously you're lying." "Have you seen a shrink?" It had always been carefully engineered (it seemed) *not* to happen when anyone else was around – again not unlike a rather bizarre movie script wherein nobody believes the teenage heroine until Freddie Kruger slices Johnny Depp to pieces in a waterbed.

So, imagine my horror when I heard a literal squeal of tires and looked up to see a blue Camaro rounding the bend in the cul-de-sac and coming at high speed toward the park. As mentioned, the only way in was that narrow footbridge - and though it had never occurred to me that anyone would be crazy enough to drive a car over it, that's precisely what happened next – almost as if the driver were bending the laws of physics by taking an object through a space that was too narrow for its dimensions, and too flimsy to hold its weight. And yet... physics seemed to have nothing to do with it.

Suddenly, instead of two friends walking in the park, it felt as if we were two fluffy bunnies caught in the headlights. That's when the internal dialog stopped. I grabbed Diane by the arm and pulled her in the direction I had indicated earlier, and we took off running. At our back, we could hear the car rattling over the wooden bridge, and quickly emerging onto the grass. Neither of us looked back as we leapt over the telephone poles and took off running through snake-infested brambles and thorny bushes which had grown up at the back fence line of the houses next to the park.

Run. Hide. Crouch down. Pure survival mode, with everything happening in slow motion until, eventually, we made it to the street on the far side of the field, and were able to walk the long way back to my house. Now - the other odd thing is that the only way out of that cul-de-sac would have meant the blue Camaro would have to pass by us... but it never did. When we got back to the house, we immediately got in my Mustang and went boldly and somewhat angrily cruising down to the park with the intention of seeing where it might have been hiding. But the tire tracks of the blue Camaro went right up to where we had jumped over the telephone pole... and then they simply stopped.

Because the grass was thick, lush and wet, it was quite obvious it had never turned around. The tracks just *stopped*. That experience is one of those things that still hangs in my mind as absolute validation of the machinations of the unknown. Not to mention - a damn good exercise in stopping the internal dialog and running for your life.

Many years later, I spoke to Diane about the experience, wondering if perhaps it may serve as some sort of clue or guidepost to the actual art of meta-magical creation. If we could so easily summon a blue Camaro, could we also perhaps summon a cure for cancer, a doorway to another dimension, a million bucks? I will admit I've tried to use the same technique for summoning my Other. "If Orlando comes walking up that driveway, I'm going to go out there and grab him!"

No, alas, he has not come walking up the driveway. I do not have a cure for cancer. The doorway to the other dimension remains elusive, and if I had a million bucks I would be living in Oregon by some craggy shoreline facing the stormy sea.

My intent has not faltered, only strengthened. So I can only look at events such as these and wonder what the catalyst might have been. Did I foresee it, did I create it, or am I really on the Shore Leave Planet from *Star Trek*? (It could happen.)

Recapitulating the Weird
Shamans, Madmen and Things That Go Bump In the Night

July, 2007

> *The shaman is the self-healed madman.*

———

Before the seeker can fully embrace the concept of the authentic self, there is a time-period and a process (I reject both words, but there they are) during which it's important to really examine who we are, what has shaped us, and why we are seekers at all. Why are *we*, unlike others around us, not content to be mommies and daddies, bakers and bankers, doctors and lawyers, complacent with the convenient distractions of the world around us? Why are *we* seemingly never satisfied – often more interested in the shadows than the warmth of the sun, more captivated by the mysteries of the night than the bright promise of the day, more compelled to chase after the muse and the mystical nature of dreams than to curl up with a good book or tune in to the latest drivel on the dogma box?

Sometimes – often – it is because we allow ourselves to *see* the things most others choose *not* to see. We are the weird ones who have seen the UFOs and the apparitions in the attic and heard the voices of spirits and angels, maybe even demons. Of course, to say they are spirits or angels or demons (or voices at all) is to draw erroneous conclusions in an attempt to wrap our humanform mind around something not human at all – but because that's human nature, it's what we do, at least until we begin to understand that a lot of what we experience is rooted in the sixth and **seventh sense** instead of the usual comfort zone of the original five physical senses.

Without ever signing on for it, we are the seers and the visionaries, the shamans and the sorcerers, the conduit for Knowledge that passes from the **place of silent knowing** and into the human world.

Throughout my life, I have been blessed or cursed with weirdness - depending entirely on one's point of view – which brings me back to a statement made earlier with regard to this path and how it changes one, with or without one's permission.

As a child growing up at the edge of a bayou in a run-down motel in central Florida, I remember lying awake in bed at night during the hot, hot summers, listening to the call of the whip-poor-will, and wondering at the mysteries out there in the dark, where children were forbidden to go after sundown. I felt neither small nor insignificant, nor did I feel invincible or immortal. I was simply myself, not attached to the name my parents had given me, not locked into any identity or idea of myself, just an androgynous wild-child who had no idea how uncivilized she really was until teachers and peers began attempting to correct her thinking and align her with the consensual agreement.

I did not know at the time - perhaps around the age of six - that it would be an altogether futile attempt. And in hindsight, I celebrate that realization. Rambling thoughts here on the other side of the continent - 3,000 miles and 40+ years from that old motel that now lies in ruins, with a sinkhole where the house once stood and the lush Florida creeping vines having covered even the crumbling foundations of the cottages where I once played and often hid from a tyrannical father.

At the time, I could not know how strange I was in the eyes of others. While schoolmates talked of Brownie meetings and the adventures of Dick and Jane, I was hiding in a stand of wild banana trees down by the bayou, watching The Strangers who passed through our property with some degree of regularity. Usually The Strangers were men - mysterious and even ominous perhaps, but never unfriendly or harmful. My mother never saw them, but my father did - and he was forever warning me to stay away from them. And yet, in a way I cannot define, I knew The Strangers were not there to hurt me... and at the same time, I knew they were there *for* me. They were there to be seen. They were there to *be* Strangers.

Two of The Strangers stand out in particular - one in a blue shirt, the other in tan, just walking through that isolated vegetable garden as if they belonged there... and perhaps they did. There was something about them - a glow, a vibrance, a mystique that did not cling to ordinary humans. I remember them as if it were yesterday, and that alone tells me there was more to them than might meet the eye. There is no explaining this, even from the vantage point of many decades of hindsight. And so I remember it only as one of those "weirdnesses".

When I was ten years old or so, I woke in the middle of the night to see a transparent man standing in the doorway between my room and my parents' room. I've written about this previously, so for now I will simply say that this "man" was very real - in the sense that he could be perceived and he was obviously perceiving me in return - but he literally had the appearance of what we normally envision as a ghost. He simply stared at me for a minute or two, and then he vanished as if he had never been there at all.

Because the attempts by my parents, teachers and peers to assimilate me into the consensual agreement had been having some minor success at that tender age, I had almost allowed myself to become convinced that "it was just a dream" when, about three months later, the man appeared again - and this time when I had not even been asleep, and so there was no possibility it was a dream. Just a little girl and a mystery sharing an eye-to-eye stare in a haunted house at the edge of the bayou.

I have never forgotten that unspoken conversation - and whenever I find myself feeling lost or indecisive in my journey, I remember those encounters in the middle of the night in the backwash of Time, and I know now what he was trying to tell me without ever speaking a word. "The world is not what you have been taught to believe." Whoever or whatever he might have been - whether some mysterious manifestation of Orlando, or an ally, or a projection of myself from the now into that dim personal history - what matters is the legacy of the experience itself. The world is nothing like we think. I do not believe it or wish it were so. I *know* it because I have Seen it, and experienced it, and that Seeing has become Knowing.

Sometimes, something will niggle at me - a sense that the consensual agreement has crept too close, a sense that ordinary awareness grows stronger in the summer months, when the days are longer, and the sun burns away the mysteries of the previous winter, and autumn lies sleeping in a future still distant on the horizon.

So it is often in the summer that I most need to remember those intimate encounters with the infinite, the unknown, the flip side. It is when the sun is at its hottest and brightest that I find myself back in a night several years ago, when I awoke at 3:38 a.m. and walked from one end of this old house in the desert to the other, only to discover that 42 minutes had passed. And - foolishly - I could have convinced myself I had simply looked at the clock wrong had Wendy not said to me when I returned to bed, "Why were you gone so long?" To this day, I have no concrete answer, though the incident itself created an awareness which has made it clear that it was not the first time, nor the last time, when the inexplicable 42 minutes have gone missing.

I found myself thinking about those 42 minutes again recently - entertaining the thought that entire lifetimes could have been lived and lost in those 42 minutes. Occasionally, I have had glimpses - just fragments of fragments of memory - into what occurred during that interval of missing time... and yet perhaps it isn't what happened that matters nearly as much as the fact that *something* happened. More than once, but often involving the exact same interval of missing time. The world is nothing like we think. I know this now.

And then there's the altogether inexplicable phenomenon of memories-that-never-happened. Events that track exactly like real memories - not dreams or memories of dreams or daydreams or fantasies. But events that we remember even though they never occurred in linear time. There are several of these "memories-that-never-happened" that continue to haunt me. The earliest is when I was no more than 12 or so, and involves a memory of myself walking down the road where my school and my church were located across the street from one another. In this "memory", it is the middle of the night and I am mildly afraid because there is no moon and it is extremely dark. I am thinking that I have just come from the church, where some type of clandestine meeting had taken place, and my sense is that I had been there with several other kids my age, and we had been "taught" something... except this was no ordinary Sunday School lesson.

I feel the pavement - uneven rough gravel - beneath my feet, and I see lights shining through the paned windows of some of the houses I pass by in this little rural town. At one point, car lights appear in the distance, but I intuitively duck behind a tree until the car passes. The details of this memory are vivid, precise and linear - not at all the same sensation as remembering a dream. It was a real event... yet it cannot be placed in linear time or fundamental logic, because where and when I grew up, 12-year-old girls were not allowed out to wander the streets at 3 a.m. And yet... in the somewherewhen of the infinite, I have no doubt that this event was altogether real.

What does it mean? Who's to say? But I am coming to suspect that what I said before is even more true than we might imagine: it doesn't matter so much what it *means*, but that it *happened*. Moreso: what matters is that it *can* happen - and it is through those cracks in the agreement that we slowly but surely come to realize...

The world is nothing like we think.

And yet, in the course of living and working and going through our daily lives, there is a tendency to get caught up in the machinations of the agreement - and therefore meditation and recapitulation become matters of reminding ourselves of what has been shown to us by the Infinite time and time again. When we forget the mysteries, we condemn ourselves to the prison of stagnation and sameness.

There is a crack between the worlds, and sometimes the Infinite sneaks a tendril through that opening to hook us onto the path, into the ultimate journey that is the revelation and evolution of the Spirit itself.

It would not be possible for me to list every weirdness in my life. And yet, there is value in remembering, in contemplating certain events from the past that have had great impact on us.

One of the opening paragraphs of one of my earliest forums, *The Shaman's Rattle*, reads:

> The journey began in 1988, when I met a man I knew to be something other-than-human. Evolved? Immortal? At the time, I could not have said and would not have believed the Truth had it been revealed to me. It was through his influence upon my life that I was forced to ask the first question: Who Are You?

What I have never discussed at length is that this was no random meeting. With deliberate Intent, I had summoned this "man" from the Infinite itself - and yet, it is true that I would not - *could not* - have accepted the Truth had it been revealed to me at that time. Despite my own Intent (which I did not yet fully understand at that time), I was still stuck in the concept of linear time, and the religion of Rationality; and since I had already decided what was Possible and what was Impossible, it stands to reason that when he initially came into my life, I ignored what I knew in my heart, in favor of what I wanted to believe in my head. In other words, the Infinite Unknown was standing right in front of me, solid as a rock and sharp as a blade, and I was too bone-headed to see it.

Maybe that no longer matters, because I did eventually embrace the journey as a direct result of this "random" meeting - and it was as a result of Do-ing the journey that I came to recognize this "man" as my double – what Castaneda called the nagual man, which is, in a nutshell, the energy body manifested, the vessel of awareness which has the potential to continue beyond this mortal lifespan. Impossible, of course. From the perspective of ordinary awareness, some would say it is even insane. "He was just a man." "It was just a dream." "It didn't really happen." And all the other mantras used by phantoms to ward off the frightful realization that the reality they pretend to inhabit is not nearly as secure as they like to believe.

"Reality is malleable." A statement made to me through the voice of gnosis. I've seen proof of this more times than I can count, yet admittedly I still look back on some of the events described above, tilting my head like a confused puppy, and saying to myself... "Nah... that didn't just happen!"

And the reality is that as long as we believe that, the belief itself becomes truth. As long as we believe the Other is just a metaphor or allegory, there is no room in the energetic structure of space-time/matter-energy for the Other to manifest in any form - because as long as we are using our energy for maintaining belief, there is no room for experience.

Just words trying to wrap around the slippery tendrils of the Infinite. It has been said that the Infinite is the unknowable - yet I might amend that to say that it is unknowable until we give ourselves permission to Know the impossible, and to experience the indefinable.

What we think of as reality is often only a precarious agreement within a vast but unstable consensus. It is only when we finally _see_ it that we empower ourselves to create and inhabit a much larger reality, free of man's descriptions and agreements. In order to finally embrace the authentic self, we learn to accept our weirdnesses right along with our mundane accomplishments – for those anomalous tendencies and experiences are often the conduit to the Infinite, the experiences that define and shape any true seeker, and set her apart from the domain of matter and men, while simultaneously giving her the ability to be the walker between the worlds – at home in either, slave to neither.

That's the true definition of freedom.

You sail lunar winds
on an ice crystal pirate ship,
one hand on the wheel of destiny,
the other full of stars.
Sometimes they drop,
seeds of eternity
scattered by invisible wings
in the loneliest garden
of visions without end.

PART TWO

Folly

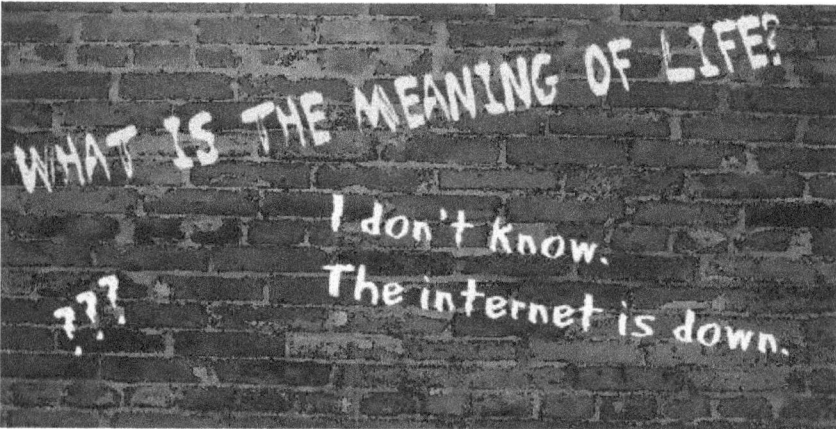

Assuming the seeker reaches the point of embracing the authentic self, after a brief respite during which she pats herself on the back and writes her resignation speech to The World At Large, there comes a time when she begins to confront the realization that the world is not only not what she has been led to believe, the world is also an irrevocable pain in the ass.

Finding the authentic self didn't make the bullshit go away! Finding the authentic self only opened ones eyes to the further realization that one has now stepped in it!

You alone are real in a roomful of mannequins, harlequins, jokers and jackasses.

Welcome to the real world...

Now what?

Words of Warning
(Offered on the advice of two advance editors)

An introduction to Folly

What's important to understand about folly is that it's virtually impossible to understand folly. We're walking along through life, thinking the world is what it appears to be... and then one fine day for reasons we may or may not fathom at the time, something happens that propels us from seekers to seers. The blinders are ripped away, and we find ourselves face to face with a world that is not only alien, but irrefutably hostile and absolutely insane if one looks too closely. Can't run away because there is nowhere to go, can't hide because all the good hiding places are already taken, so we forge ahead.

That's what seekers and seers do. Only when we really see the world for what it is and what it isn't do we gain the ability to see *beyond* the world of matter and men, and into the realm of the seventh sense – the world that lies beyond the veil of illusion which has been pulled down over our eyes since before we were born.

The problem is, the process of having those blinders ripped away is never easy, and often ugly. For me, it occurred when I underwent what is commonly called a shamanic initiation. This process was described at length in my first book and on the *Quantum Shaman*™ website, but bears a general recap here for new readers. Essentially, I was journeying with the ally when my double came face to face with me, tore me asunder, and then proceeded to sew himself inside my skin. Though this is a common experience among shamans of all cultures, the result was that it changed my view of the world and my experience of that world forever. I could no longer pretend that the false belief systems and consensual agreements were right, or even sane. I *saw* the world in ways most would choose to never *see* the world...

and yet for the seeker who commits to this path in earnest, there is no denying or skipping this part of the journey.

What follows in this section are the rants on the walls of my soul – my dark and often angry view of the destruction of my previously well-ordered world. I hope some it if is amusing, even if only ironically, but it is deeply honest regardless of how it may be received. Read with caution, and with the knowledge that this, too, is part of the warrior's path – one more step on the journey toward wholeness.

Before a new world can exist, the old one must fall.

This is the fall.

"If Only You Could Be More Positive!"
What if your authentic self is an asshole?

It was sometime in the vicinity of 1992, shortly after we had sold our house in San Diego and moved to the desert that some old friends came up for a visit - three women I had met in the course of my *Star Trek* writings, and who – for reasons unknown to me – had taken upon themselves the task of attempting to make me more presentable to the world at large. They meant well, I suppose, and yet in the big picture, their motives were purely self-serving. Put another way – they wanted to groom me to be the next "queen bee" of their clique, and the harsh reality was that I wasn't interested in the least... but they didn't know that, and perhaps I didn't know it myself.

At first, it was almost flattering. As Sally Field once exclaimed at the Academy Awards, "You like me! You *really* like me!"

Maybe they really did like me. Who's to say? But it all began to go south when I started hearing phrases like, "If you could just smile more when you're in public!" "If you could just pretend to have an interest in Mary Jane's thimble collection." "If you could just be more positive!"

Hmmm. Though this was just before I embarked earnestly on The Path, I was starting to hear the voice of the consensus reality in ways I had never quite heard it before. These women didn't like *me*. They liked an *idea* of me – and with that in mind, they were quite willing to invest a fair amount of time and energy into the chore of molding me into their idea of who they *wanted* me to be, with little regard for who I actually *am*.

Took me awhile to realize that. And it was an ugly truth when I did. What they were *really* saying was that I did not live up to their expectations. I'm not really one for walking around with a big, toothy grin. I really don't give a rat's ass about Mary Jane's thimbles. And frankly, if I wanted to live life behind those rose-colored glasses, I'd be wearing an orange robe and handing out flowers at the airport.

So there I stood in the middle of my life, face to face with the abrupt realization that my authentic self was a bit of an asshole – at least when measured by the expectations of the ladies' sewing circle and terrorist society.

Maybe that was a turning point in my life, in the sense that it caused me to examine who I really am, and what I was willing to do about it. Did I want to be accepted by these women because they had flattered me? Would I be willing to put aside my own identity in favor of trying to be what someone else wanted or needed me to be? And, at the end of the day, did I even *want* to fill the niche these nice ladies envisioned for me?

No, to all of the above.

I see that now with great clarity, but at the time it gave me some sleepless nights, for the simple reason that we are so programmed to *need* to be needed, to *want* to be wanted, and to *love* to be loved... even if it means giving up who we are in order to attain those things we have been led to *believe* we want... when the reality may be that we don't really want them at all.

I must admit, I tried to try on the identity for awhile. Tried to be more positive. Tried to care about thimble collections and take an interest in these folks, with whom I had about as much in common as a Martian would have with a marigold. In short, I was pretending. And in very short time, I was miserable.

Fortunately, it wasn't long after this that we began receiving communications from Orlando, and I was able to ask him why I had failed so miserably in my bid to "just be more positive."

He actually laughed at me. Said, "A bat may put on a dove's wings, but she's still a bat when all is said and done."

I was offended. Doves were better.

He gave me that look, then. "Says who, and why do you believe them? Instead of trying to be something you aren't, why not simply be the best at what you *are*?"

That was the day I took the most deeply cleansing breath I'd taken in years. That was the day I put my dove back in the box. And that was the day I finally accepted myself, unfurled my black leather wings, and said with total acceptance of the consequences: *"I-Am!"*

Of course, it's not that simple. Before we can accept our place in the world, we have to truly *see* the world for what it is. Sometimes we laugh. Sometimes we cry. Sometimes we scream – because at the end of the day, we find ourselves scratching our heads and wondering why the hell everybody *else* doesn't see it, too!

More importantly, we cannot begin to embody the change we seek until we acknowledge with abject clarity that the world is a nuthouse and the lunatics are running the asylum. What does the madhouse look like? Something like this, perhaps.

One of the three women who came to my house that day revealed a few months later that she was going to visit a psychiatrist and, in her words, "...pay him to convince me I want to have children." She had always been an independent woman who had expressed that she did *not* want children, but when pressured by husband and friends, she was willing to abandon *her* identity for the picture inside someone else's head. If that's not a portrait in the attic of the madhouse, I don't know what is. I truly hope she found her happiness, or at least managed to upload the *idea* that she wanted children, because there is nothing worse than finding oneself in someone else's play on a stage that has no exit.

The night is a black book
written in invisible ink,
full of alchemy recipes.
Between the pages
obsidian orchids are pressed,
staining the tissue paper sky
with a pollen of stars.
When all the blooms have fallen
like angels from heaven
I will be no closer to death.

The Evil Butterfly of Interconnectedness
An Exercise in Folly

September 15, 2004

Got home late last night from a long weekend of work. Detached the cargo trailer from the Suburban, had a bottle of water, then got back in the car to take our employee home, some 35 miles away. Was contemplating the idea of interconnectedness. Flow. Flow. One into the next. All into the each. Each into the other. Harmony and soft melodies swelling through a forest of tall pines where a young virgin blows kisses to a white unicorn. Ain't it all grand?

Well... this morning I woke up and realized I needed something that was still in the heavily-loaded car. Ah, but in order to move the items I needed, it was necessary to first unlock the trailer to search for the dolly, which entailed finding the keys (which had been put back in the wrong place), and that meant stopping everything I was doing to initiate The Search. Once found, I unlocked the trailer to discover a veritable mountain of manna scrambled into a pile of rubble because the load had shifted in the 500 mile trip, so that meant methodically unloading each little trinket and putting it back in its place. This took about an hour in the desert heat until such time as I finally came upon the one item I had been searching for - the invaluable 2-wheeled dolly.

By this time, my meditations on the subject of interconnectedness had begun to take a dark turn. I scowled, but continued with cussed diligence, muttering under my breath about the requirements of impeccability and the need to erase self-importance. Wiped sweat from brow. Rolled dolly back to car, only ran over foot once (which required a trip to the head for a bandaid) and then realized that the items in question were buried underneath "The Fragile Stuff". Thinking again of interconnectedness. The dolls are connected to the fairies which are on top of the glass baubles, and isn't it lovely how it all forms such a splendiferous mountain of meaningless folly, but nonetheless is interconnected to my ability (or seeming lack thereof) to accomplish the *one* single task I set out to do in the first place.

In the course of making 25+ trips in and out of the house to unload each thing in accordance with its nature to break, scratch or suffer terminal damage (Note to Self: "I don't do delicate!"), I noticed that the path to the storage room (formerly known as the guest bedroom) was blocked by still more stuff which had been left in a state of disarray by a well-meaning employee. This was discovered quite abruptly when, while carrying something that obscured vision, I tripped over aforementioned chaos, banging shin severely in the process - another trip to the head, another bandaid, then back to the storage room to face the original disarray, plus the added bonus of all the stuff dropped when leg was nearly fractured. Cleared path, took deep breath to cleanse the spirit, inhaled large amount of dust, sneezed violently, wrenching neck in process. *grumble grumble interconnectedness my ass*

Finally unloaded the two tubs from the car, but before I can get them in the house, the phone rings, so must run to answer the call; and the cat is giving me that look that says she's going to do something foul if I don't change her box *right now*. The one normally-flat surface in the house (the bed) looks like two bigfoot mated there, and before I can use it to sort through all that fragile stuff which is now being carried around by the weenie dogs, I have to strip off the sheets and throw them in the wash 'cuz some 4-legger barfed on the comforter, but there's a huge box on top of the washer which has to be moved first, which means throwing the sheets on the floor (can we all see this coming?), and that means tripping over them in the dark hallway. Another trip to the head. No more bandaids, the gun is out of bullets so can't shoot self, and by now the cat has reached the end of her patience and, yowling triumphantly, has deposited a token of her displeasure on the floor somewhere in the general vicinity of the litter box, but not exactly in it.

Another deep, healing breath - serious mistake. There is a devil. Cat crap is proof. My eyes water, blinding me to the table which has been moved in the brouhaha. Stub toe, thinking fondly of the butterfly flapping his wings in China to create a storm on the other side of the world, and by this time I'm seriously considering squashing the pretty little fucker with a fly swatter, because all this interconnectedness is altogether true, but not all the sweetness and light it's cracked up to be. That butterfly is the incarnation of pure evil.

By now, the weenie dogs are yapping for breakfast, but there's no dog food in the cupboard because the house sitter didn't bother to go to the store as instructed, nor inform me he hadn't done so, so that means a trip to Wal-Mart... in the car... that is still heavily loaded... with all that junk... which is interconnected to the last nerve... which is seriously frayed and beginning to unravel like a strand of cheap beads.

Ohm.

———

I Am...
mortal dust dusting the mirror,
fleeting paradox casting
eternal reflection.

Granny & Gabriel
"There's a special fire..."

April, 2001

As a child growing up, we lived with my grandmother who was senile more or less from the time I was born. My memories of her consist primarily of her sitting on the porch in a rocking chair, literally waiting for Gabriel's horn. While waiting, she sang old hymns and talked in a 3-minute repeating loop, where her entire existence could be summed up in these experiences which were all that seemed to remain of her memory. I'd come home from school, ask how she was doing, listen to the loop, which always concluded with, "And now I'm a-sittin' here, a-waitin' for Gabriel's horn."

Being a somewhat devious child, I had an instinct that she wasn't as daffy as she was trying to get everyone to believe, so one afternoon I crawled underneath the porch with one of those plastic flutofones from 3rd grade music class, and just as she was praying for Gabriel to sound his horn... well... I let 'er rip! Next thing I know, I hear a clatter and a howl as granny topples over backward in her rocking chair, feet up in the air like some deranged cartoon character, and all the while praying at the top of her lungs, "Jesus is coming! Jesus is coming!" as she tries to scramble up and right herself lest Jesus might catch a glimpse of her size 10 bloomers which had been revealed when her dress flew up over her head.

Needless to say, when I crawled out from under the porch, I wasn't the most popular kid on the block with my mother, but when I locked eyes with Granny and she realized that Gabriel was none other than her toe-headed granddaughter, there was a new understanding between us. From that day forward, she had more lucidity when talking with me privately - she really *could* carry on a conversation beyond that 3-minute loop, though she would fall right back into it whenever anyone else entered the room. My guess was that she was bored with life and bored with the lives of those around her, and so she was creating the reality that had been far more real to her - those 3-minutes of memories when she was really Awake, Aware and Alive (the 3 "A's).

Once, a few years before she died, I asked her what she really thought when she heard that horn sound. She just smiled. "There's a special fire just for you," she said, shaking her bony finger. "The devil has a *special* fire, just for you."

White picket fences are only cages
and all the world's a coffin
floating down a river of stars.

The Dysfunctional Family Christmas Play

Have a holly-folly Christmas!

Circa December, 1999

Every once in awhile, I find myself faced with a situation that genuinely vexes me, despite everything I have learned and experienced on this path of Knowledge. One of those situations happens every year about this time, and can best be encapsulated with the words, "The Dysfunctional Family Christmas Play." Now, before I go any further, I should warn you that I am not much into Christmas these days. So if anyone is expecting a cheery and uplifting Christmas tale of power, you might want to stop right here and go rent *Miracle on 34th Street*. Also, be it known that I'm not really looking for solutions to the problems I'm going to talk about, because it is wholly recognized that there aren't any. I just have a need to spew out some observations, and let them be whatever they are. Naughty or nice or somewhere in between.

There has been a rift in my extended family for some years which was long ago deemed beyond resolution. Both of the primary players in the drama are perfectly okay with that, but other family members simply insist on doing The Dysfunctional Family Christmas Play regardless of the fact that having the two primary players in the same room is rather like attempting to have matter and anti-matter in the same container without any dividers. As Mr. Spock could tell you even without a tricorder, an explosion of universal proportions is inevitable, entirely predictable, and - note - *also entirely avoidable by not introducing the volatile elements into the same physical space at the same time.* It's a no-brainer. Just. Don't. Do. It.

What is it about the holidays that makes people go through the motions of something that is entirely unreal 364 days a year, yet they want to *pretend* it's real on that one special day? I sit in a restaurant as a captive audience to the

97

off-key blatherings of, "*Santa Claus is Coming to Town*," and I hear myself muttering under my breath, "Would somebody shoot the fat bastard at the city limits so we can all get back to our *normal* dramas and pretenses?" (Yes, I was Ebenezer Scrooge in a past life – or Orlando was.)

On the other hand, Christmas is a wonderful time for *really* observing the play in motion, because it comes to the surface far more than on any other occasion, with the possible exception of a large Baptist funeral complete with paid wailing women. In my own situation, we had been invited to the usual family gathering, with the understanding that it would be a group of five, and the "rivals" would not be present. This is the way it's been for several years now, everybody is a lot happier, there is far less stress, and if it ain't broke, don't fix it. So, we agree to the invitation... and after the plans are set, it is *then* revealed that "the rivals" will be invited. Now... here's my gripe. The wording of this revelation (a private email) is such that if we say we are uncomfortable with it, we are then ogres who must be treated accordingly. We are instructed to be "grown up" and essentially told to "get with the program" – when, of course, getting *away* from the program is what we've been doing for years. On the other hand, if we go, it is walking into a stressful pretense that couldn't be any *more un*pleasant than radical chemotherapy. I ask through gnosis what is the solution if I decide to go, and gnosis responds, "Just be yourself."

Hmmm. To do so would come with some rather dire consequences, because if I *did* go and was "myself", I'm quite certain I would end up telling The Fam exactly *why* it is dysfunctional, why that will never change, and offering a rather untender suggestion for where they might want to put all that cheery wrapping paper.

What is it about the illusion (and it *is* an illusion in this case) of "one big happy family" that will make everyone go out of their way to be miserable for the entire month leading up to this magical day (magic has a dark side, too), when in the long run, the characters in a Looney Tunes cartoon are more real by comparison? I don't really want or need that personalized fat-gram-counter from "the rivals" anymore than they want or need a roll of toilet paper printed with the likeness of hundred dollar bills. The whole thing is nothing more than warfare concealed, and though some would say the holidays are about healing rifts and forgiving past grievances, I would say, in a single word, bullshit. That's just one more program running in the background - this strange guilt-and-manipulation-driven program which tries to tell you you're the original Uncle Scrooge if you don't really care to suck up to family members who turned their back on you when you needed them most.

But for the sake of a few Polaroids to stick in The Dysfunctional Family Christmas Album - if you'll look closely, you'll see Aunt Sara leaning awkwardly away from Lecherous Cousin Fred; and Brother Joe rolling his eyes just as the flash caught him with his hand on Cousin Jack's ass; and the constipated grimace your mother-in-law is trying to disguise as a smile - an entire group of people who might otherwise be happy and peaceful in their own right spend a lot of time stressing out over what to get for their estranged sister, or what to say to the uncle who molested them when they were six, or rehearsing whatever clever line of dialogue they intend to burst into the room with when the door springs open and the unseen director in everybody's head shouts, "Lights, camera, *dis*satisf-action!"

At Christmas more than any other time, I can see why don Juan told Carlos that he had to get away from his family and friends and set out on the path of being unknown. Perhaps in some warriors, there is still a need or desire to interact with the bearers of one's DNA just for *auld lang syne*, but for the most part, as I observe the machinations of it all, I can only feel what can best be encapsulated with the words, "Nobody can take their eyes off a sleigh wreck."

Who Died and Left Me In Charge?

September 19, 2004

I do not like the sound of my own name. It isn't just the modulation of it as it hits the air - which is entirely neutral, just a series of grunts and clicks signifying this monkey instead of that purple elephant - it's the fact that nine times out of ten when I hear my own name, it is immediately followed by a recitation of problems which would best be resolved by a quantum physicist in possession of a time machine and matter re-arranger.

Last winter while I was in Florida visiting me poor ol' mum, I received a call from one of the folks with whom I co-own the house in which we all live. The conversation began, "Della, we have to get a new roof or our insurance company is going to cancel us and bad things will happen."

Hmmm. I'm 3,000 miles away, and instead of calling a qualified roofer, he calls me. So I go through the song and dance, informing him of a handy device called The Yellow Pages, which may be found in the top drawer or on the internet, and further instruct him in the fine art of getting three estimates before settling on the first dude who shows up and wants you to hand him $50K in cold hard cash in advance. Then, at the end of the phone call, I took my poor ol' mum to Disneyland, and went about my life.

That evening, there were at least three emails which began, "Della, where is the phone book?" "Della, there is no listing in the phone book for roofers." (Well, duh - then try looking at "Roof installation" or "Roof repair", or "Gee, can I find my ass with both hands and a map?")

This went on for three months. Even long after I had returned to California, I assumed the matter was being handled by "Jack", who had taken it on as his pet project. Well... it was only a few days before the insurance was scheduled to be renewed or cancelled that Jack came into my office and said, "Della, what are we going to do about the roof?" I could only stare blankly at this man, mentally calculating prison time that would result if I just snapped and strangled him. Nothing had been done because, apparently, his name wasn't Della. ?!?

I made a few phone calls (in self-defense at this point), and the roof was installed within a few days. *But...* there were problems, as could be expected when having to contract for a major job at the last minute, and now - almost nine months later, the battle continues with attempting to get the roofer back out to correct it. Once again (foolishly), I told Jack to take care of it. Gave him all the phone numbers, contact information, contractor's license number, and everything he would need to set it all in motion. I should mention that I am out of town on business a lot, and Jack is at home, so if appointments need to be made, it stands to reason that they have to be made by the person who is going to have to be here when the workmen show up. Despite my super-human abilities, I have yet to perfect the magical art of being in two places at once, even with a cell phone and a laptop!

Last I heard from Jack, the roofer was supposed to show up "tomorrow" and fix the problems. That was a month ago, and - silly me - when I heard no more about it, I figured it had been handled, because I was out of town for nearly a week when that "tomorrow" came and went. This morning, I was awakened by an odd flapping sound coming from the vicinity of the roof. Crawled out of bed, padded through the house in my bare feet, and climbed up the ladder to see yet another major section of the roof flopping like a fish out of water in the brisk pre-autumn winds.

As I was coming down the ladder, I encountered Jack standing there with that look. "Della," he begins, causing my lip to curl and my sphincter to tighten, "the roof isn't fixed."

Grrr. So... I am really beginning to wonder who died and left me in charge? Last time I checked, there had been nothing on the news to indicate that everything in the world (my own world or anyone else's) which must be fixed, repaired, installed, painted, tiled, buffed, washed, cooked or cleaned had somehow become the responsibility of "Della".

"Della, the UPS man is at the door."

"Della, are you going to cook dinner tonight?"

"Della, the cat crapped in the corner."

"Della, the roof just blew off and a cackling woman in a black dress is circling the chimney."

Fuck it. I'm going to change my name to Dorothy. That bitch had it easy by comparison!

Hobby horse shadows gallop the sand,
broken free from the carousel clock-face of time,
driven by the whip of vampire wind.
Moonglow bleaches the night grey-white
and on the jagged mountain horizon
a rainbow comes and goes,
there, then gone,
eyeliner on the faces of angels
who shed falling stars like feathers.

Chaos Conspiracy Theory
"I tried to read the instruction manual, but it's written in Chinese!"

November 26, 2004

Over the past few weeks, I have been going through what I can only think of as a rewriting of Chaos Theory in my own head. It goes something like this:

I logon to Delphi yesterday and see my "signature" has lost its pictorial background. So I futz around with it for a couple of hours, figuring it must be my problem, only to later discover this is some sort of "new and improved" inner gazurkis on the Delphi servers designed to create a more enjoyable atmosphere for... ? Who? And how? But no matter.

So I go to the help forum, only to be directed to another help forum with my problem. That forum tells me I am not allowed to post yet, and that I must return in one hour. They did not specifically tell me to bring back the broomstick of the wicked witch, but I suspect what will be next. Luckily, I *am* the wicked witch of the west, and carry a spare with me at all times, so shall present it to them (you can guess which-end-first) upon my return in one hour. /end Delphi rant

So then I logon to eBay to do some maintenance and relisting, only to discover that eBay has likewise switched overnight to the new and improved eBay. This translates to the fact that my ads which had been designed to fit within their parameters are now falling off the page and require left-to-right scrolling in order to be read, and if you're like me, you probably don't even try to read something where that's the case. Again, figuring it must be my problem, I futz with it for hours, until...

Finally get on the phone to tech support, where I am on hold for over an hour listening to some over-enthusiastic robot on puppy-uppers chattering in my ear about stuff I already know or don't want to know. Endlessly. Without cessation. To the point of bone-diddling madness. When the tech finally comes online awhile later, I am informed that the engineers have made some "improvements" (?!?!?) and we all just have to live with it. In other words, I now have to re-write HTML on over 200 individual ads so as to comply with the new and improved eBay which doesn't work fer shit, when it was working just fine before this grand new installation of Chaos Software Incarnate. /eBay rant

The bottom line to all of this seems to be that the world is rushing forward at some great and hectic pace in some bizarre notion that it is improving things, when the reality is that I used to be able to go into the supermarket, have the nice lady check my items through by punching the price into a cash register, and I was in and out in half the time (literally) it now takes for this new and improved technology to scan, process, inventory, and otherwise examine and categorize every individual piece of lettuce down to the nth degree of minutiae.

And don't get me started on the wrapping on a CD or DVD! Remember the good old days? We bought an album (remember those, kiddies?), brought it home, slit through the cellophane with a fingernail, and put the damn thing on the spinner. Behold - let there be music in less than 3.5 centuries! Now? Just yesterday, tried to unwrap a new DVD, and one would've thought the remains of Jimmy Hoffa were stored in that hermetically sealed wrapper. The labyrinths of Tut's tomb would be more easily penetrated! By the time I finally got the damn thing out of its sixteen layers of protective seals, wraps, locks and casings, I had forgotten what movie I was trying to watch, not to mention my own name! The men in the white coats were standing outside with a butterfly net, because I must've called them, or else my cell phone became sentient and dialed the number all by itself - which it seems to do quite frequently, keys locked or not, just so I can get a nice surprise of lots of long distance calls I didn't make... thankyee very much!

And then let's talk about the cell phone itself. Maybe it's just me, but why does it seem I have to go through a series of commands more elaborate than what would be required to launch this country's entire arsenal of nuclear weapons, just to make a call? I just want to say hello to me poor old mum, not remote control the entire resources of Starfleet from the palm of my hand!

Life used to be simpler, didn't it? (Yes, I do know I sound like my grandmother). I mean - seriously - is this part of the reason the world seems to be spiraling faster and faster into some irredeemable abyss of confusion, conflict and technological incompatibility? The DVD player can't read the CDs which are compatible only with the 'puter, and the MP3 is mating with the iPod, and the VHS is sitting lonely and lost and obsolete in the corner even though I bought it less than six months ago, and the workmen in the living room are trying to measure for carpet using some sort of laser-sighting gizmo which can't seem to get an accurate reading because of the glint on the window; and they've been there for over an hour screwing around with it, scratching their collective heads... so I went and got my tape measure and informed them it was precisely 30', 6.5" in width, by 30' 6.25" in length. Close enough for jazz and government work, boys?

So my personal Chaos Theory is this. It's all a grand conspiracy hatched by the hive mind in an attempt to so thoroughly distract one's energy and monopolize one's time with absolutely inane folly and trivialities that we have no time or energy left to pursue the things that really do matter - like our own spiritual well-being and evolution. The longer we are on hold, the longer it takes to open that wrapper or wait for that price check lest the world economy be thrown out of balance on some computer, the less time we are spending on our own individual pursuits.

I could go on. But I won't. I'm going to go fix my lunch with an old-fashioned slice of bread and some tuna, eat it with my bare hands, and lick my fingers clean when I'm done.

The rest... is just chaos.

Life Among the Wal-Martians
"Yes, Virginia, there are zombies."

November, 2004
The Day After Thanksgiving

When I was a little girl growing up in the middle of
nowhere in the middle of Florida in the middle of the 1960s,
things were different (she said with a drooling, toothless,
cackling grin). Well - things *were* different. Thanksgiving was
different, to be sure. No stores were open. Not a single one.
Anywhere. There were no fast food joints back then, and
when they did start springing up in the late 60s, they weren't
open on Thanksgiving Day. Or Christmas Day. Or even New
Year's Day.

The world stopped, paused for at least 24 hours, and then
slowly started back up again the next day, though a lot of
businesses - including many retail stores - were closed for the
entire Thanksgiving weekend. I recall even as recently as 10
years ago, trying to find something for lunch while we all
waited for the turkey to cook. Drove around Poway to
deserted streets, a drizzle of rain, maybe one or two other
hapless, hungry souls on the road, and finally found a gas
station open where a tiny deli was serving sandwiches.

This morning, I had the misfortune of actually needing
something legitimate at Wal-Mart. I should state for the record
that we live in a relatively small town. Wal-Mart is the only
major store in our area, otherwise it's a 45 minute drive into
Palm Springs.

Wanted to go to the store early this morning - not to
indulge in some bizarre ritual known as Christmas shopping,
but to pick up some things I actually need in the course of
living my life. Like cat food. And bread. Can of paint.
Would've gone out at 7 a.m., but had to wait for a workman to
show up. He never came, of course. This, alas, is also different
from how I remember the world. Used to be if someone made
an appointment, they either kept it or called to say they

couldn't. Now, they just don't show up. So I finally just left, but by now it was later in the morning and somebody had left the gate open to Zombieland, and the phantoms were out in full swing, looking for some nice juicy brains to eat, because one thing was patently obvious: they didn't have two brain cells of their own to rub together, and the air whistling between their ears was producing a vacant, glaring glow in their lifeless eyes.

Not a single parking space in the Wal-Mart parking lot. That alone was scary enough, but what it signified was that all those Zombies were actually in the store. With strollers. And geezer-pleaser-power-chairs. And screaming babies. And sneezing/wheezing sickos spewing the latest and most virulent cocktail of flu germs because they are simply too self-indulgent and self-important to stay home and avoid spreading those germs which have already resulted in a flu epidemic.

Nope. Somebody somewhere told them all they must go out today because, after all, it is the day after Thanksgiving, best and busiest shopping day of the year, and even if they don't have a dime in their pocket or any clue of what they might want or need, by ye gods, they *will* be in the stores with that vacant, hollow, consumerized stare, because that's what the program calls for, amen, hallelujah, jeezus christ is born, with Christmas carols blaring on the loud speaker, and Silly Sally Wal-Droid shouting over the PA system in a high, squeaky, obnoxious voice, "PRICE CHECK ON REGISTER 375! WILL SOMEBODY PLEASE GIVE ME A PRICE CHECK FOR SUPER MAXI SOAKERS WITH FLUFFY ANGEL WINGS!" that someone who doesn't understand the language would swear she was hollering for a full evacuation in light of a possible terrorist attack rather than just trying to get some overworked, underpaid, kindergarten drop-out to go look at the shelf price for a bag of rags, which the embarrassed young Marine husband has now kicked to the floor and is loudly proclaiming, "Those aren't mine! Honest! I don't know how they got in my cart!"

Three babies in opposite corners of the store have become possessed by demons, and are screaming at the top of their tiny lungs, while two old ladies are fighting over the last Christmas-tin of 3-flavor popcorn, and eventually end up dropping it on the floor, where the lid flies off and the contents spew forth like so much holiday confetti, causing the two ancient bats to lock up like a couple of Sumo wrestlers while belting out a string of profanity that would curl the toes on The New and Improved Anatomically Correct Transvestite Ken Doll.

As Mr. Garrison said on South Park: Merry Fuckin' Christmas!. If this is any indication, it's about as merry as a woman who's just caught her husband in the garage with the neighbor's pet sheep.

Gives a whole new meaning to holiday fruitcakes.

———

Is it just me?
"What part of no-workee do you not understand?"

August 3, 2005

Woke up yesterday morning to discover the DSL connection wasn't working. Waited awhile, but finally got on the phone to the service provider. At first, a recording informed me that their website would be most helpful in troubleshooting problems with DSL outages. Should have taken that as fair warning. But I waited diligently on hold until a perky tech came on and asked the nature of the problem. Told her several times in several manifestations of language - "My DSL isn't working. I have no internet connection. Computer no workee."

After being instructed to unplug this connection, reconnect it here, disconnect that thing over there, and stand on one foot while whistling Dixie on the armpit chorus, the perky little tech tells me, "Okay, now I want you to go to our website so we can troubleshoot some other things."

"Computer no workee," I repeated. "DSL is down. Internet connection kaputz. Can't go to website if computer no workee."

"Well, yes, but from the website we can determine the precise nature of the problem based on a series of questions."

Was this girl deaf? So I repeated my woes. "DSL is down. Internet connection nonexistent. *Enterprise* plunging into atmosphere. Scotty dead, and no one left to beam me out of here."

I don't think she ever really understood. Kept insisting that I go to the website even when I was telling her the DSL was nonfunctional. Good thing I wasn't trying to troubleshoot a toilet. Could get ugly. And deep.

By mid-afternoon, temperatures had soared to over 100 degrees, and the monsoon season had taken its toll on my patience. Sweating is for race horses and clammy-handed Baptist ministers who always want to pat me on the arm. I do not find sport, honor or pride in sweating, so when the swamp cooler abruptly gave up the ghost in a fit of screams that sounded like demonic laughter, I immediately picked up the phone and called The Elusive High Desert Repairman. Was told by the first guy that he could send someone out on an emergency basis in 2 to 3 weeks. The next guy's phone was disconnected. The third guy had an answering machine that played Dueling Banjos. Guys number 4 and 5 had "gone a'fishin". Guy 6 wanted me to take the motor out myself, bring it to his shop about 30 miles away, where he promised to have it running again in a couple of months. The rest of the jolly band of misfits either didn't answer at all, had been shut down for non-payment of bill, or did not speak English.

When I lived in San Diego, this was *not* the norm. If I called someone who had bothered to place an ad in the yellow pages, chances were they answered their phone and sent someone out within the day. Imagine that - a business that actually shows up, solves the problem, takes my money, and hands me a receipt on their way out the door.

I am convinced that 99% of the "workers" of today are inorganic zombies, created and hatched by the pods in the savage garden of entropy.

Aliens have eaten my roses and a rattlesnake I encountered on the road last night said he was late for a very important date, as he tipped his tiny top hat and slithered off the stage to make room for the next nonsequitur.

The rabbit hole has fallen into itself and the serpents have eaten their own apples.

The shadows have sharp edges tonight,
jagged cookie cut-outs
splintering the delicate hymen
between your world and mine.

Depression, Clarity and Phantoms
"If it ain't broke, don't fix it!"

February 20, 2006

It seems to me that what the consensus calls depression may be the direct result of what a warrior calls clarity. I'm thinking of depressed housewives and stock brokers hurling themselves off the Sears tower. Both see the futility and the folly in the world, but have no sense of guidance to turn their clarity into personal power. That's the difference between warriors and phantoms. The problem is - even warriors can fall prey to depression if not extremely vigilant and aware. That's when clarity has become the enemy - we literally *see* that the world is a nuthouse, but we fail to realize that we are *in* the world, but not necessarily *of* the world.

Usually when I feel depression coming on, it's telling me I need to take a look at something in my own matrix - *Why* is it affecting me? Yesterday was hell, for example, because of consensual programs infringing on my personal space and time. Started out with trying to get in touch with the phone company, only to get one of those chipper robots who wanted to "help" me. After twenty minutes talking to a daffy machine, I was finally connected with "the party best suited to serve my needs", only to be told it was a 1.5 hour wait due to heavy phone traffic.

I was furious at first, ranting and raving and asking, "What's wrong with this fucking world?" I call the phone company, only to talk to a robot for twenty minutes and then be expected to hold for another hour and a half! Don't they make enough money to hire more people? It *literally* took that robot twenty minutes to determine who would be best qualified to serve my needs, when a receptionist could have done the same thing in twenty seconds!

What amazes me is that the powers that be don't see what is obvious. I frankly don't know *anybody* who would wait on hold for 1.5 hours, and if they *do*, they are pathetic sheeple who must be seeking companionship from that robot who babbles in one's ear for the duration of the hold time - dealing out such mind-numbing repetitious platitudes as, "You're our *favorite* customer! So please continue to hold while our highly trained executives finish up their 3-hour lunch with their mistresses, and our technicians are out on a smoke-break. Your time matters not to us in the least, so we feel completely justified in wasting it! But you *are* nonetheless our favorite customer... because you're *dumb* enough to just put up with it and never complain."

...and all in a smarmy sweet voice that makes me want to get an AK47 and go postal. Ah, such sweet fantasies of robot parts scattered all over the pavement, oil black like blood in the moonlight, mainframe CD ROM cybergazurkis splattered on the walls with such artistry that even the investigators from CSI would have to pause and reflect on the sheer beauty of the kill.

So, yes, the world is a nuthouse, and the robots are directing traffic in the asylum. My patience for it wore thin and ran through the cracks long ago, so now when I get one of those robots, I cut to the shortest path to leave a message, and then I just start screaming - as a stalker, with full awareness of precisely what I'm doing.

I figure a calmly worded message simply won't get anybody's attention - so while they're laughing at the loony shouting on the answering machine, maybe at least one person will get it through their head that this *was* a customer who is no longer a customer, and actually suggest to upper management that maybe giving the receptionist her job back would be a more energy efficient move than software maintenance for some expensive cyberbimbo.

If it ain't broke, don't fix it. If it *is* broke, fire the asshole who broke it and try again. The handwriting is all over the walls, graffiti on the subways of Hell. Somebody really needs to start reading it to figure out why we have so much road rage and anger management problems. Maybe - just maybe -

it's because we're all tired of being treated like a boil on the ass of all those companies who claim they want to help us.

Get mad and let them know why. As long as people are sheeple, it's only going to get worse. We have the power to create reality in *all* aspects of life. Reminds me of that old, old movie, _Network_, where a news reporter just snaps one day, and goes ballistic all over the airwaves. At one point, he's hanging out of a window in New York, literally screaming, "I'm mad as hell and I'm not going to take it anymore!"

I resemble that remark. And I second that emotion. And I am writing this while *on hold*, waiting for tech support.

The Biggest Cult of All
"Forgive me for not asking for forgiveness."

April 16, 2005

As I was at a mall in southern California recently, I was a bit surprised to see a Christian clothing store. Eh? Holy Jesus on a t-shirt! Really weird stuff, too - some of it so graphically violent with all that nailed to the cross stuff, and the blood and the depiction of ecstatic agony... If it had been a movie, it literally would've received an NC-17 rating for all the gore, but instead it seemed to be almost a sexual turn-on for the two pubescent girls standing in front of the display nudging one another suggestively.

At first, I tried to dredge up the tolerance bone, but sometimes I really do think "tolerance" is just one of those buzz-words that goes a long way toward letting a lot of weirdoes get away with a lot of weirdness, and really doesn't have much to do with actually learning to get along with one another. To tolerate someone tends to imply they are doing something essentially intolerable, so tolerance is one of those words I've been studying of late.

As I'm walking past this store, the glazed-eyed zombie-girl dripping with crosses and wearing an artistically ripped shirt proclaiming, "I am the door," smiles her zombie-eyed smile and says, "Jesus would love it if you were to come in to the light!"

I felt like I was being asked to step inside a cult - which, of course, is precisely the truth, even though one generally thinks of cults existing in obscure alleys or zombies at the airport or anywhere *but* a brightly-lit mall in San Diego. I've often said that the Catholic church is the biggest cult in the world - the only reason it's acceptable is *because* it is big, and so it's hiding in plain sight. Think about it. If your kids came home from school and said they wanted to go to a meeting where they would be asked to drink the blood of a dead man who was fathered by a ghost and born of a virgin; eat the flesh

114

of his resurrected corpse; and that if they were accepted into the club, they would be symbolically drowned in a river of blood and raised from the dead by a child-molester in a white sheet... you would probably think twice about letting them go, eh? But because it's a "legitimate" church most people fail to really see just how bizarre all those belief systems really are. Almost makes Heaven's Gate and Jonestown sound sane by comparison.

Point is, what I found disturbing about the store at the mall was that our current society has made it cool (and profitable) to be a religious zombie. The store was full of rosy-cheeked teens piling Jerseys for Jesus on the counter, and whipping out mom's credit card while the register sang the sacred hymn of cha-ching, cha-ching, cha-ching.

Couldn't help wondering... What would Jesus buy? Hmmm. Perhaps that roll of designer toilet paper on the back shelf - the one with Satan's likeness embossed on every sheet, bearing the scripted verse, "Get thee behind me, Satan."

The destruction of faith is the beginning of evolution. Amen to that.

Faith makes us docile
in the face of our own death.

Ironies of the Phantom Planet
"Klaatu Barada Nikto"

October 31, 2005

I do not believe we are indigenous here. We are the only species who must strap rags to our bodies and dead animals to our feet in order to live in any sort of comfort. The red tailed hawk who flew in front of my vehicle yesterday - so close I could look into his eyes - did not need a sweater to ward off the chill, nor reading glasses with which to see, nor road signs to tell him the cardinal directions. The coyote who crossed my path at dusk ran wild and free, without concern for whether it was 5 p.m. or 6 p.m. according to daylight savings time, and though he was running helter skelter through jagged rocks and dense brush, he required no rough-terrain Nikes, and no wife or husband to cook his dinner so that he might eat.

"It's a simpler life." Those words whispered through my mind on the dusk of Halloween, when the shadows from the mountains to the west had long since swallowed up the wilted sun, and the tumultuous winds had blown away everything except the lone vagabond walking at the edge of the road, carrying his tattered backpack and shielding his eyes with a leathery hand from the swirling sand. In one way, the coyote and the man were no different, and yet I couldn't help thinking that one seemed to belong here on this Earth, and the other was some sort of strange interloper who could not survive in the wild except for the technology of his species.

As I bumbled along alone in the motor home, high on cold meds that had turned the road into a strange grey glass snake on which I was riding bareback, I coughed once or twice, snuffled, and then gave a verbal snarl at the irony which had led to my currently sorry state of health. By and large, I am quite healthy despite minor aches, pains and deteriorations that go with getting older. Being exposed to the public as much as I am, I get the occasional cold, but with a few

116

precautions and awareness, I had managed to remain cold-free this entire season.

So how did this one come on? Through irony, of course, and a chain of interconnectedness that is both inescapable and yet also inescapably annoying and even frightening. I have this cold right now because I had a toothache almost a year ago. "Eh?" you say. Well, it goes like this...

Woke up in the middle of the night with a sensation not unlike someone driving a red hot poker through my bottom jaw and up into my skull. Turned out to be a bad tooth, though there were no physical symptoms that could be seen externally. No cavity, no crack, just pain that was reproducing itself exponentially every 3.5 seconds. By the time I could be seen by a dentist (several days later, even for an emergency appointment!), the dentist was shocked to discover that my blood pressure was "deadly high." Well... duh? The bitch has been in searing agony for 4 days while the dentist has been on the golf course, and though the vicodin has been a fine ride, it has done absolutely nothing to ease the pain, and so it stands to reason that the reading on the blood pressure monitor was more along the figures of the national debt.

So after being told it would cost $4500 to save this one little tooth, it was highly recommended that I see a medical doctor to get the blood pressure down immediately, because (and I quote) "We here at the dentist's office can't risk treatment with your blood pressure so high!" And, never mind that the primary reason it *was* that high was from being in pain for four days and counting.

So in self defense, I had to go to another witch doctor in order to get the first witch doctor to help me. (Note to self: next time, tie string to tooth, other end to truck, have Wendy drive forward...) But no matter. When I go to the Doc in the Box Clinic, they are indeed alarmed that the BP is so high - despite the fact that I'm telling them the saga of being in pain for so long. The doc says he can give me something to bring the BP down, but uses the leverage of saying, "But I can only give you a seven day supply unless you have this blood work that might show us *why* the reading is so elevated." Grrr. Ain't it obvious? Lemme kick you in the nuts every 7.2 seconds for four days, and see how *your* blood pressure is reading at the end of that time!

By this time, the pain has taken its toll, and so I agree to the blood tests - which reveal nothing in particular, save for a sluggish thyroid. In a way, I was almost glad to have that news, since it explained the weight gain, blah blah blah. So... the doc puts me on thyroid meds, gives me the script for the BP medication, and sends me on my way, telling me to come back in three months for a re-test. Fine - tooth may now be dealt with, BP quickly drops back to some semblance of normal, and all is well. I even go back in three months, am given a new script, and sent on my way again. Fine. Doc even says he's got the med levels where he wants them and I'm starting to drop some pounds. Yeah.

...'cept when the script runs out again and I call in to have him refill the drugs, I am told by the snotty receptionist, "We can't do that. You have to be seen." I tell her I can see myself just fine, all is well, and that I would really rather avoid a visit into the clinic because every snuffling imbecile within a 50 mile radius is sure to be in the office dispensing germs like Jesus freaks handing out pamphlets at the mall, and since I am clearly doing fine - and no blood work is required - could they please just renew the script over the phone with the pharmacy?

Of course not. You must be seen. The phantom menace cannot grok that this is not only unnecessary, but entirely unethical if considered in light of "the right way to live". There is no real reason for me to go to the office, yet if I want my drugs, I must be seen. It is like a mantra, so often repeated that it has lost all meaning. Attempting to reason with a doctor's receptionist is rather like arguing with a bull moose with a hard-on. You're going to get fucked, no matter what you do.

So finally I make the decision to go into the office, and sure enough as I step through the door, I am greeted with half a dozen snuffling, sniffling, coughing, wheezing patients who never heard the news that there is no cure for the common cold, nor even the flu, and therefore going to the doctor for same is rather like going to McDonalds in search of a left-handed monkey-wrench painted fluorescent green. One child is running around the office, a mobile virus factory, hacking and sneezing as the wind from his body fans the germs through the air with the same efficiency as if they had been injected straight into the vein. Other patrons glare at the unconcerned mother - who is reading a copy of *Parenting* magazine - but even a gentle reprimand to the child by an elderly patient goes unheeded. Little Tedley is a perfect darling, we are told, and nothing must be done to stunt his creativity - even if that creativity includes drawing satanic symbols with a black crayon on the walls at the doc in the box while his head spins around backward and he spews green spittle down the front of his "Little Angel" t-shirt. Children are only good with ketchup.

Though the appointment was for 9 a.m., I am not "seen" until after 10, which means I have now been exposed to a full hour's worth of Other People's Maladies, and my being seen consists of walking in to the exam room, a quick BP check, and then the doc says, "Why are you here?" Drugs, I tell him. Thyroid junkie. Remember me? He barely looks at me, writes out the script, and sends me on my way.

... and like clockwork, three days later, on Friday morning of our last show of the season, I am hit with a cold that comes on like a freight train, but may be traced directly to a toothache that occurred almost a year in the past.

When I stand back and really look at the irony of it all, I can only feel a strange sense of futility that comes from truly knowing the world is Insanity's private playground. The very profession that tells us to avoid exposure to colds sets up its practice in such a manner as to insure maximum exposure to anyone coming through the doors. The dentist can no longer simply repair a tooth, but must cap it and crown it and root canal it until the bill more resembles the defense budget.

While some forms of interconnectedness may offer a sense of comfort, this type of seeming dependency on the phantom world is both disheartening and deeply disturbing in so many ways. It has always been my feeling that if we go looking for monsters, we may find them - and that is ever so true with the medical profession. But don't get me started. For now, I am simply contemplating "the simpler life" of the coyote and the hawk and jackrabbit in my back yard, who is feeding on shiny green shoots of grass brought up by the last rain.

If there are aliens on this Earth, we are them. Not only is the species primarily mad, but the madness does indeed appear to be contagious.

Oh... and, of course... can't take the thyroid meds with cold meds, so the final irony seems to be that the very thing I went into the doctor to get is rendered useless because of the thing I received. Ah, the interconnected ironies of the phantom planet.

Perhaps it is no wonder that shamans shed their clothes and dance naked in the moonlight and howl at falling stars and smear plant extracts on their bodies to cure ailments, or imbibe mushrooms to induce visions of Otherworlds where the human madness has not yet spread. In a crazy world, it seems the only sane thing to do.

Some mornings it just ain't worth gnawing through the straps.

Enter Lock Code
"Everything I say is a lie."

May 4, 2006

In the middle of a rough day in Los Angeles yesterday, I picked up my cell phone, only to discover that it had become possessed by the ghost of electronic demons and was now reading: "Enter lock code." Since I have never locked the phone and never had a lock code, I could only stare at the funny little screen - which never ceases to remind me of Captain Kirk's communicator - with a combination of dismay and amusement. Enter lock code.

Oooooooohhh! Made me feel like a secret agent on some grand mission to thwart the likes of THRUSH (anyone old enough to catch the reference is congratulated on still being on this side of the dirt). But then it really began to sink in that this strange device for which I pay a handsome fee each month had essentially locked itself behind its electronic wall of despair, entered its cyber padded cell, and no amount of coaxing or crying on my part was going to change that. I turned the phone off, back on again, entered "logical" numerical sequences at random... all for naught.

Enter lock code.

The muscles in my neck had begun to tighten. My hands were starting to shake. In a public place in downtown Los Angeles, perhaps it would not have seemed odd in the least had I danced naked and called upon the slathering servants of the sanguinarian order, but since various and sundry homeless folks perform such rituals quite often (and seemingly to no avail - since they are still homeless and half mad), I resisted the urge and proceeded to try to call the phone company on its own device. Foolish attempt. But we do silly things when confronted with silly realities. Enter lock code. No surprise there.

This morning, after some amount of digging through user's manual that bears more resemblance in weight and thickness to The Complete Encyclopedia of All Things, I finally happened upon the entry that is supposed to solve all my problems. "Locking and Unlocking the phone." With a great sense of relief, I performed the required functions... Seventeen missiles at NORAD launched. The entire network of communication satellites in orbit over the earth realigned and began playing *Who Let The Dogs Out*. Space aliens appeared on the White House lawn to protest the disruption of old reruns of *I Love Lucy*.

But that little screen still persists: Enter lock code.

Called the Verizon store where I bought the persnickety little pest, only to be put on hold for fifteen minutes, and then cut off without so much as a by your leave. This happened not once, not twice, but five times. Seems the hold function has a time limit, at which point the mortal fool waiting on Line 1 is cut loose over the abyss and plummets to the death of her senses while the robotic voice continues to assure her that her call is important to the megalomaniacal corporation who still has not hired a receptionist, and is clearly not aware that the call is so important that it is set on a 15-minute cut-off. Yes, I timed it. All the while staring at the little screen which reads: Enter lock code.

The password to my eBay didn't work. The combination of my old locker in high school proved fruitless. The DaVinci Code failed.

By this time, I had grown a rather serious set of fangs and my eyes had begun to roll back in my head as is common with sharks when they feed. So when the ditsy blonde at the kiosk finally answered the phone to inquire, "For whom are you holding?" it required a monumental effort of stalking on my part not to turn her into virtual lunch. She was *not* associated with Verizon Wireless, of course... just a humble grunt who promised to connect me... but never did.

When I was finally able to talk to the manager of the store - never *did* get through to the phone company (who seems not to have a working phone) - his brain trust suggestion was,

"Why don't you just bring it down to the store and I'm sure we can take care of it for you?"

Lemme see. It's an hour's drive, with gas at $3.55 per gallon. How's that for a "why not bring it down to the store"? Gee, I have a cell phone so I *don't* have to show up in person to solve the problems created by the cell phone.

Do we *need* all this stuff? I ask myself that question at least a dozen times a day. The digital clock on my brand new stereo cannot hold the time for more than 36 hours before it starts flashing 12:00 in blue neon numbers bright enough to light the entire state of Vermont. The security system on the car takes it upon itself to shut down the engine if the proper drive code is not entered in a timely manner. The computer turns itself on and off like a cheap hooker on a busy Friday night, and there's a 6-foot rabbit running around my living room complaining that he was accidentally beamed down from the *Enterprise* due to a glitch in the reality filtering system that separates then from now and here from there.

Enter lock code.

The Medical Profession - Wankers and Bozos!
Go ahead – ask your doctor!

October 25, 2010

Is it just me, or is the medical profession comprised of the biggest bunch of bozos and wankers ever to come down the sewer pipes? Went to the doc a few weeks ago 'cuz I was having chest pains - probably related to my back, also probably related to the stress (what? me? stress?) that accompanies running one's own business in an economy that has been programmed to decline and continue to decline even when there is (and I quote a respected financial analyst) "not much logical reason for the continuing deterioration." But no matter... The world is a nuthouse and the lunatics are running the asylum, so... nothing new there.

Chest pains, I say. So the doc stares at me for awhile, doesn't even offer to listen to my heart to see if I'm dead or alive, then starts writing prescriptions for the most expensive drugs on the market without so much as a by-your-leave. "You are a diabetic," he reminds me in his thick accent, as if that should explain so much for so many at a time when it seems to me that "diabetes" is the fad diagnosis of the 21st century in the same way ADHA and MPD were the fad diagnoses of the '90s.

Put another way: he is telling me to behave like the label he has stuck to my ass, and gets uppity when I remind him that I am neither a label nor a dis-ease. I am a person with a name and a life partner and a cat and a dog. I am not just a "diabetic" - and with good reason - for once we become labeled by our handlers (doctors, lawyers and charlatans of all walks of life), we become to them nothing more than the label itself. And let's face it, folks. Diabetes is the cash cow of the decade! Walk into any Wal-Mart or Rite-Aid or the like, and you will find not just a small shelf of diabetic supplies, but an entire aisle consisting of a cornucopia of products designed to put a smile on any CEO's face. So keep in mind that when your doctor tells you you're a diabetic, what he's *really* seeing is not your potential well-being or lack thereof, but a long line of checks in the form of kickbacks from the pharmaceutical companies - who *knowingly* market products which have more side-effects than potential benefits. Any doubt, do your own research. I did - and I was appalled!

Ask your doctor. Go ahead.

Maybe it stands to reason that when I came out of a store yesterday and glanced at the newspaper racks, there was a glaring headline which read something like, "Diabetes expected to triple by the year 2050 - 1 in 3 will have the disease!" Be afraid! Be very afraid! Run to the priests of the prescriptions and ask your doctor about all those yummy drugs that are just as likely to kill you as to cure you. Wear this label! Act out your dis-ease! Be a good patient! Play your role!

Role. You're in a play, you know. We all are. Yes, including your doctor, who probably knows a lot less about your body than you do. A few months ago, one doc tried to schedule me for a prostate exam. ??? That could get interesting.

Here's the thing, folks. And this is *not* the exception to the rule near as I can tell. In 2004, my mother had 2 colonoscopies, both of which returned normal results. She died in 2006 of colon cancer, which had been present for years according to the medical examiner's final report. In 2008, my ex-husband was diagnosed with scabies (bugs, to the uninformed), and subsequently treated with expensive skin care products. The reality? His gall bladder was enlarged to twice its size, and gall stones had torn up the bile duct - *none* of which showed up on MRIs, blood tests, or the like. By the time he got a correct diagnosis and had the gallbladder removed, he had suffered severe damage of the bile duct, lost over 80 pounds, and was wandering around town in a confused state because of the resulting toxins which had built up in his system. Several years ago, a good friend went to the emergency room complaining of abdominal pain so severe she couldn't stand and could barely breathe. She was told to go home and take a laxative and an enema. She died a week later of peritonitis, caused when her impacted bowels ruptured.

Need I continue?

Why on Earth or any other civilized planet do we trust these clowns, when it is proven time and time again that they kill more people than they cure? Enough already! I go in with chest pains, and the doc gives me a prescription for pain pills and muscle relaxants! About 18 years ago, when I went in with a large lump in my breast, I was told by the first quack, "I'd recommend ignoring it for awhile and see if it goes away." Arugh! What?

The bottom line is that *we* give these gonzos the power of life and death over our bodies - and it's high time we stopped just buying into their sweet-scented bullshit. So today as I was sitting in the waiting room of the lab - for over 2 hours, I might add - I found myself looking at the downtrodden, frightened people waiting to be told whether they would live or die, whether they would be asked to play the role of a Diabetic or a Heart Patient or a Cancer Victim.

I happen to like Dylan Thomas's view on it:

> *Do not go gentle into that good night,*
> *Old age should burn and rave at close of day;*
> *Rage, rage against the dying of the light.*

Maybe it's all just a crap shoot. Society tells us we will die of something, yet this is the same society that once told us the earth was flat, and at the center of the universe. So maybe it's time we stopped buying into the programs, turn off the idiot box that keeps trying to sell us on this or that drug and encouraging us to "Ask your doctor about mycoxafloppin..." and go back to living the way nature intended:

Eat well.

Run when the lion comes out of the jungle.

Love unconditionally.
Get fucked often (and *not* by the medical profession!)
Take back your power.

ADDENDUM: Approximately 2 months after writing the rant immediately above, I suffered a heart attack and was subsequently admitted to a well-known hospital in Palm Springs, where I was promptly advised that I would require a triple bypass three days before Christmas, or, in the words of the ghoul in the surgical gown, "You'll be dead in two weeks."

It is now more than 2.5 YEARS since that time. Having done my own research to confirm that bypasses really do not save lives as they are purported to do, except in the most extreme of circumstances, I am still on this side of the dirt and doing remarkably well. A change of diet, more exercise, and willful intent.

Do your own research, people! Do not be led by the nose to your grave because the doc's wife needs a new pair of tits.

Life in the Fast Lane
The Generation of Entitlement

September 15, 2004

Something is wrong with the human race. Obviously a lot of things are wrong, but for today I'm just going to deal with one, which might be best described as living in the fast lane.

In the course of our business, we work renaissance faires, and also have a business on eBay, plus our website. Now, for the most part, folks who go to Ren faires are pretty laid back, often spiritual or hippie sorts, who don't make a lot of demands. That's a good thing, in my book. I go to the faire, set up our booth, and then it's organized chaos for a couple of days, before we tear it all down, put it back in the box, and head home to regroup before heading out again the next weekend to do it all over again.

The problem lately has been coming home, for there is no rest, only more work. As I wrote in a recent journal entry, just trying to unload one single item into the house turned into a fiasco 10-layers-deep, under the general heading of, "But you have to do *this* before you can get to *that*." And yet, the more I do, the deeper the hole goes. There is no digging out from under the rubble, because the more one digs, the deeper the hole becomes, and the more rubble falls on one's head.

Within the past 48 hours, I have also observed an interesting trend, which is actually the focus of this long rambling rant. Living in the fast lane. On Monday, a young man wrote me wanting two items from our website, but he wanted them in his hand by Thursday. I emailed him back promptly, telling him one of the items was out of stock, and unless he wanted to pay overnight shipping, there was no way I could get the second item to him within the timeframe specified.

But he writes me again the following day, asking the exact same questions as if he never received my email - even though his inquiry is now attached to the two previous emails. Could

128

I somehow get these items to him by Thursday? Out of stock or not, wasn't there some way I could have it drop-shipped to him from the warehouse? He would pay extra, he promised, but he really must have these items by Thursday or worlds would end and entire civilizations would fall on his head. Gotta have it. I could all but see him literally hopping from one foot to the other like some coke-stoked speeder who needed his next fix. Had to have it.

It's not like we sell medical supplies or anything that anyone really needs. Baubles and trinkets, tapestries and bells. Trust me - nobody needs this stuff anymore than they need a tattoo on their left testicle.

I again dropped him a polite email, telling him it couldn't be done - because by this time it was Wednesday morning, and even if I might have been able to get to the post office, it suddenly occurred to me that I was done jumping through hoops. The moment of realization was quite profound. I took a deep breath, shook myself off the way a dog shakes after a long swim, and looked around. Nothing had changed, except I was beginning to acknowledge that I really don't want or Intend to live my life according to the demands and fast-lane-madness of Other People. If he really needed these items by Thursday, could it not have occurred to him to order them a couple of weeks, or even a week in advance? Where did it state that it was my responsibility to run across hot coals in order to accommodate his poor planning? - yet this seems to be the manner in which a lot of businesses run. One of my competitors on eBay offers "shipping within 2 hours of receipt of payment." Yeah - knock yerself out, buddy. When you get to the end of your life and ask yourself what you did while you were on Earth, you can tell yourself you were the fastest shipper in the west, and you ran yourself into the ground - literally - doing it. The gravedigger ain't gonna give a fat rat's ass.

I should point out that this is not uncommon. At least a couple times a month, some turkey writes me in a dither because, "My wife's birthday is tomorrow, and I need you to overnight this doomaflodgit or that hootem to her in Bangladesh - and, by the way, could you gift wrap it and run to the store to get a nice card to go with it while you're at it?"

Er... no, I can't. She's your wife, not mine.

Within the past few years, I have felt what I can only describe as an unrelenting sense of urgency - a sense that the world is in a constant hurry, but it doesn't even know where it's going, and so the results tend to be rather like a herd of mindless lemmings in a hurry to hurl themselves off a cliff just because the asshole in front of them can't stop in time, and it's a 6-billion lemming pile-up at the bottom of the bottomless abyss.

Maybe I'm just getting old. But when I was a youngster (she said with a toothless, drooling smile), we simply weren't in that much of a hurry for anything. But when I was growing up, it was a different world, and in some ways, I think it was a better world if comparisons can even be made. When I got home from school, there was no mad rush to get to soccer practice or ballet lessons or gymnastics practice or anything. I was a kid. I went outside and played - and it was magical! Running headlong through dark orange groves with mystical beasts of my own creative imagining chasing me or assisting my quest.

I had time to just _be_ - and I'm not sure people under the age of 30 have any idea what that really means. When I was in my teens, there was no pressurized angst to get to the mall (*gasp* - malls hadn't even been invented yet!), nor did I feel compelled to have the latest cell phone, the most "awesome" computer (*gasp* - computers and communicators were only real on Star Trek at that time), nor did I have any particular desire to have my own car (*gasp* - because, living in the country, there was nowhere to go anyway!) So I made my own worlds. I learned to dream and to imagine. I learned to write, yet now I notice that most people can barely read, and that's another indication of the deterioration of the human spirit, for obviously we live in a world of words and ideas - but it is a world that becomes increasingly closed off to those who don't know how to use even the most basic tools.

The reason folks are so depressed, so stressed, so overworked and spiritually and socially *lost* is because they have lost touch with a more natural human "rhythm". The problem is that I have often made the mistake of thinking this is the "occasional" day of chaos - but the reality is that every day is chaos. It's how we live our lives, and it's not healthy on any level. But we all just smile and nod and go right on putting the pedal to the metal with the cell phone in one hand, the Starbucks in the other, the Whopper in our lap, and one elbow on the horn while shouting, "Get out of the way, asshole!" out the window of the mini-van while the kids are plugged into their iPods in the back seat, oblivious to the fact that they are living, breathing organisms capable of incredible things. We are more than our ability to absorb input from the world around us, but that is fast becoming a well-kept secret in this world of more stimulation, more titillation, more aggravation. We are losing touch with the core of what it is to be human.

The best birthday gift I ever received was a book. When I unwrapped it and found all the pages empty, I gave my mother a weird look, wondering if it was all some terrible mistake. There were no grand adventures, no pirates or witches or vampires or words of wisdom. Just blank white pages. She only smiled. "That book is the story of your life," she explained. "Take the time to write it well."

Sound advice.

Chaos Theory... *STILL* Ongoing. Or...
What makes you think you get to do that?

January 30, 2006

About a month ago, I had to call the local coppers because some little twerps who live in the meth house not far from here (and this is considered a *nice* neighborhood!) decided it would be perfectly all right if they were to ride their dirt bikes not only up and down the street (illegal in California), but also onto my property where the fence was demolished in the last flash flood. The funny thing was that they weren't even discreet, and seemed to think it was their inalienable right to pilot these noisy, dust-raising vehicles anywhere they so pleased. I wondered then... what makes you think you *get* to do that? The law seems to say one can ride one's dirt bike 24/7 on one's own property. Fine - but this isn't their property, nor is the field across the street, which has been practically destroyed by such activities that tear up the fragile desert topsoil, destroy vegetation, and create a dustbowl which the rest of us must breathe because some half-baked little junkie *gets* to do that?

Over the past two weeks, I realized I have been waking up like clockwork between 3 a.m. and 4 a.m., unable to go back to sleep. At first, thought it was just a weird sleep pattern, but a few nights ago, I realized I was hearing what amounted to a low-grade "heartbeat" of drumming. Turns out, our new hillbilly neighbor seems to get up at that time of night, turns on his car stereo loud enough to be heard in Los Angeles... and again I wonder... why does he *get* to do that, when it is clearly disturbing to anyone not already stone cold deaf?

And let's not get into the whole thing about testosterone-poisoned little jerks who have those boom-boom stereos in their car. There have been at least three or four incidents in various drive-throughs where the noise is literally so loud from the car behind me that the McDroid can't hear my order, and when I go to pay, it's like having to learn sign language just to create a work-around for the little asshole who *gets* to do that. About two weeks ago, I finally just snapped. Stuck in the drive-thru with some shaved-bald-headed gangster playing his bass so loud I thought I would literally have a heart attack from the vibration (yes, it was *that* bad), I actually got out of my car and went to confront him - something I am not usually wont to do. Needless to say, he never even turned it down to see why this crazy witch-woman was standing in front of his car, mouthing, "Would you PUH-LEEEZE turn it down?" Just showed me his middle finger. Guess that's his form of sign language. Not wanting to be impolite, I responded in kind - and added the universal gesture for "jerking off". And he *gets* to do that because, apparently, we live in a world where everyone is either afraid of the assholes or doesn't care to do anything about it.

If someone waved a knife in my face, or a gun, it would be considered some manner of self-defense if I were to beat them to a bloody pulp. And yet, if I am standing in line to go to a movie and some bimbo is waving her cigarette directly under my nose, I'm supposta just smile and nod and say, "Lovely weather, isn't it?" For all she knows, someone else standing in that line may have asthma or severe allergies that could make a cigarette as life-threatening as a gun or a knife. Yet, she *gets* to do that because our society has agreed that cigarettes are a social grace (or, more likely, because the tobacco companies really own the government at a certain level). I wonder if any jury would see it as self defense if someone were to treat an impolite smoker with the same degree of severity one might treat a knife-wielding maniac.

I grew up in a world where there was a "common sense" saying that has virtually vanished off the radar in this generation of rudesters, gangstas and road rage. "Your rights end where someone else's begin." I don't know why that is so hard for people to grok. Why do "some people" think they *get* to infringe and impose on the rights of others? If you want to ride your dirt bike at all hours of the day & night, buy a trailer and drag it out to BLM land where such things are legal and you are only disturbing some confused jackrabbits. If you want to play your music at levels that deafen every living thing within a 40 mile radius, go buy yourself a plot of land that *has* a 40 mile radius, and park your inconsiderate ass smack in the middle of it all. If you want to smoke in a crowded public place... stop and ask yourself whose rights you may be violating by doing so. Sure, you have the "right" to do all these things, but beyond a certain point, others have the right to question why you *get* to do that.

The Things We Cannot Change
Remembering the Punch Line

September 7, 2008

God grant me the serenity to accept the things I cannot change,
courage to change the things I can,
and the wisdom to know the difference.
-The Serenity Prayer

Came across this quite by accident this morning, and was reminded of some thoughts I've been kicking around in meditation. Namely - to what extent does a warrior concern him/herself with "the things we cannot change." For example - with the US elections coming up, all we seem to hear focuses on politics and political parties and platforms and all sorts of yada which is, ultimately, under the heading of "the things we cannot change." Oh, we're *told* that our vote matters, but does it really? Hell, I voted for Gore, and by all accounts, he actually *won* the election, and yet we still have The Burning Bush in The White House. So I cannot really believe my vote matters. Not one wit. If elections don't turn out the way the powers that be *want* them to turn out, there's always The Electoral College to tidy up the mess made by The Sheeple - at least that's how it seems when we strip away all the bullshit and get down to The Bottom Line.

So I ask myself... why should a warrior vote at all? All things being equal, whoever ends up in office is going to be there because that is what the powers that be will dictate. The wars of this nature are fought in places where you and I will never venture - smoky board rooms and sleazy high-dollar whorehouses where congressmen and senators go to spend our tax dollars.

But no matter - my question is simply this...

Since warriors see the game for what it is - a series of illusions strung together to create what passes for our social "reality" - why would a warrior concern himself at all with things like elections, political causes, or even global warming? I know I'm out on a limb here (what else is new), but it seems to me that these things may well be only distractions to our path. I can't imagine that Jesus would have come down off the mountain to visit the local polls, or that Buddha would have any particular opinion on McCain's running mate. These are, after all, temporary and transitory concerns - and ultimately, I *really* cannot help but think they fall under the heading... "the things we cannot change." If you think otherwise – if you feel your ire rising up to righteously insist that These Things Matter, I would suggest you take a step back and take a long, hard look at why you might believe that from the perspective of an eternal being.

I've said many times that the world is a nuthouse and the lunatics are running the asylum. The few on this planet who are genuinely *sane* see the game for what it is, and most probably end up living in those isolated caves, or in some secluded monastery where the things we cannot change have at least a minimal impact on their personal path. And, if we're going to be brutally honest here, this path *is* a selfish one; and life is sufficiently short that I can't see that I have time to involve myself in political causes which are as fleeting as a fart on the wind. Oh, we are *told* otherwise, and yet I have always sensed a sinister undertone to a lot of what we are *told* - paranoid as this may sound, I have often felt that "society" and "religion" have similar goals - essentially to provide distractions and diversions from the path, so that while we are off waving our peace signs and proselytizing for the messiah-du-jour, we lose sight of the *real* goal, which is our individual and personal evolution.

The scary thing is that this is just an innate part of the program - a built-in mechanism which functions in such a way as to weed out all but the most tenacious and ruthless warriors. May not even be sinister. May not have anything to do with sentience (and probably *doesn't*). Might just be a part of nature's design - survival of the fittest, natural selection. I've actually heard and experienced the voice of the consensus reality coming out of the mouths of people who *claim* to be awake and aware - telling us it's time to get with the program, time to grow up, time to put away the silly quests and focus on what's "real". Problem is... what's real to the phantom is nothing more than another phantom to the warrior who *is* awake and aware.

I run into a lot of talk about "global concerns," and yet I find that I simply cannot summon the energy, strength or the desire to care much. As a result, I often get chastised for being "socially irresponsible" - but isn't that just another guilt-trip laid on us by the world, one more attempt to get us to involve ourselves in things which, ultimately, we truly *cannot* change?

When I find myself being asked or expected to participate in "the things we cannot change," I am always reminded of the *last* line of the serenity prayer... the punch line.

God grant me the serenity to accept the things I cannot change,
courage to change the things I can,
and the <u>wisdom</u> to know the difference.

Economics, Politics & Panic
Who said so, and why do you believe it?

September 25, 2008

I have come to the conclusion that abdicating from the world of matter and men may be the very best thing a warrior can do - though I am fairly certain most will disagree at some level.

Several years ago, it began to occur to me that I had become segregated from the world and, as a result, from most people. At first, I experienced a small amount of alarm at this realization - I have no friends by the traditional definition, no social groups with whom I interact regularly, nor do I watch television, listen to the radio, or go to church. My initial reaction to that observation was to scold myself - "Self, you've become a hermit! Not only do you not *have* any friends, you do not appear to *miss* having friends!"

And yet...

When I was brutally honest with myself, I also came to realize that this seemingly sad state of affairs had been arrived at solely through my own choices *and* my own desires. And, perhaps worst of all, I was and *am* quite content with this. In other words, it wasn't that I had *lost* all my friends, or even lost interest in the world at large. More accurately, I have *found* that once a warrior sees through the illusions, delusions, political dramas, world wars, pseudo-terrorism, economic crises and the like, the warrior has a tendency to end up living somewhere in an isolated environment, not unlike don Juan and his little shack in the desert. And, in my opinion, that is a good thing in the grand scheme of things if one is truly serious about *Be-ing* a warrior, as opposed to just talking like a warrior.

I can honestly say that I would know nothing of the current economic crisis (oh, those fearful words!) if others had not brought it to my attention. That's one of the perks of not being plugged into the consensus reality through the

138

comforting teat of the terror-tube. Gives new meaning to the old cliché - "What we don't know won't hurt us." And, again, I'm fairly certain many here will raise the argument of "Forearmed is forearmed," or something to the effect...

Over the past few years, our business has continued to do well, even though we are what might be called a "luxury"-based business - the things we sell are definitely *not* essentials. Clothing, jewelry, little indulgences for the kiddies... absolutely nothing of value whatsoever. And obviously, those are the types of business which are the first to fail in a bad economy.

So I ask myself... to what extent does my own mindset contribute to all of this? In other words, had I been more aware of "The Economic Crisis" (be afraid, be very afraid), is it possible that my own fears would have caused me to take a different course of action, and perhaps thwart myself in the process? For example, a lot of our acquaintances in the business have said they cannot afford to restock because they are hoarding what little money they make for survival. On the other hand, Wendy and I have restocked freely over the past few months, and as a result, we have the merchandise to offer to customers, whereas our competitors may be beginning to appear shopworn - victims of their own fears.

We like to tell ourselves that awareness is always the key - and, indeed, that is a true statement. And yet... when stalking the consensus reality, it certainly seems there are times when one simply needs to walk away from the fear, turn a deaf ear to the blathering media, ignore all the predictions of doom and gloom by the analysts, and *do* the right thing in whatever one's individual position might be. It's when we start living in fear that we start hoarding - so the seeds for next year's harvest may be squirreled away for times of famine, and one has to ask, is the famine even *real* at the level where we ourselves exist? And if the seeds are never planted, where will next year's crops come from?

I've said before, with regard to politics, that I no longer vote, nor do I give a fat rat's patootie about who will end up in the white house in November. It isn't because I am an irresponsible fuck that I walked away from all of that - it's *because* of the warrior-stalker's ever-present awareness, the brutal knowledge that my vote is not going to change the world, nor is yours. Idealistically, it could be argued otherwise. But reality has proven otherwise just within the past few years.

Having clearly seen what happens when the people go against the powers that be, it seems to me that *any* investment of energy in the process of politics is entirely folly - and not the least bit *controlled* folly. Simple. Folly. Period. The ultimate no-win scenario. No matter which way you bend over, you're still going to get... well... you get the picture, yes?

That being the said, it also seems that this current Economic Crisis (run for the hills! put your money in a sock! be afraid, be very very *very* afraid!) is being played up with all the usual pomp and circumstance that precedes any major election, but may not be any more real than the gas shortage of '73 or the notion of a lone gunman in the Kennedy assassination. I mean - *really*! - what would happen if they gave a crisis and nobody bought into it? What would happen if we all just turned off our television sets and went about our day to day affairs as if none of it were happening?

Well, Della, that's a bit naive, isn't it?

I dunno. *Is* it? Are there times when too much information - particularly too much *false* information - may actually cause us to panic, and in our panic, create that self-fulfilling prophecy which says, "The sky is falling!?" Would the sky fall at all if everyone could just carry on, doing their impeccable best, rather than trying to speculate and prepare for some imagined crisis that seems to be far more of a shell game for the power brokers than anything else? We hear terms like bail-out and economic collapse and the like, but is there anything we can actually *do* about it? Pull our money out of banks and stick it in the mattress? And, what would that solve? And what other problems would it create in the big picture? Self-fulfilling prophecies are the most dangerous of all, for there is a certain grim satisfaction in being able to say, "See, I told you so!" And yet... somehow I don't think I'd feel right predicting the sinking of a ship if I then went out and sank the ship just so I could say, "See... told you so!"

The point is simply this. Do. Not. Engage.

Or, if you are going to insist on believing that your vote matters or your awareness of every detail of The Economic Downfall of America is going to somehow make you a better person, then at least try to keep it in perspective. A warrior's perspective. Which states, very simply: "In a thousand years, it won't make any difference."

Folly.

There are some who do not like to acknowledge that everything in our world is folly, because once we acknowledge that, it is a huge blow to our ego, and often a crushing blow to our self-importance. We want-to-believe we are going to make a difference, our vote will count, rah rah rah and wave the flag for freedom, but the ultimate (and ugly) reality is that we'd might as well be playing with Monopoly money and moving our little chits along the board game of Life.

A grim outlook? Hardly! When a warrior is finally able to *see* that it's all just a crazy game, there is a sense of freedom which goes beyond the ability of words to express. Sure, I still maintain my responsibilities to my life, my family and the things I care about - but I do so largely *because* I am *in* this world, but no longer *part* of this world. I make no apologies. I feel no remorse. I don't accept guilt trips. I simply do not find it beneficial or productive to care about the things I cannot change, particularly when it is so blatantly obvious that the problems which have been created at the highest possible level will not be solved as a result of me turning my attention to it.

I respect that there are many warriors out there who believe that our involvement in such things are part of the path, but that has not been the case for me, and to be honest, I'm not sure it's the case for anyone who is wholly committed to the path of self-evolution. Reason being - if I were to devote the kind of time and energy it would require to address the problems of the here and now (economics, war, famine, meth, illiteracy & people who don't know how to drive, just to name a few), I would have no time at all to devote to my own pursuits. And let's face it: when it's just me and the eagle, I'm not going to have a whole lot of concern about what I did to try to save the world. The eagle ain't keeping score, and death isn't advising me to go out and campaign for the latest joker in the three ring circus. I have more important things to do - and so do you.

So in that regard, I have to say that a warrior chooses her battles and her battlefields. When I place myself in alignment with "**the right way to live**" in regard to these issues, what inevitably comes to me is that our responsibility is not to "the world" (which is little more than a series of illusions strung together like so much holiday popcorn), but to the self, and to those who might cross our path. I have always found that there is never a shortage of problems close to home - people (and I consider animals to be people, too) who just seem to naturally come into my field of vision, and whom I might actually be able to help on some minor level.

I don't have to go out looking for souls to save or causes to engage. It's all right here - as Dorothy said - "right in my own back yard." Sure, even that is only controlled folly, but at least it may actually serve to enhance my own awareness while simultaneously serving another's, so there is some mutual benefit to the engagement, which seems to indicate an efficient use of energy - far more than banging one's head against the political arena or trying to vaguely understand or even wrap one's mind around the sum of trillions of dollars of debt.

In the 60s, there was much talk of "getting involved." Luckily, I have grown older and hopefully somewhat wiser. The only winning move is not to play.

Human Sacrifices
Warning: F-Bomb Dropped Often!

November 8, 2008

It looks at this hour as if Prop 8 has passed here in California. What is prop 8? Well, it essentially says that only a man and a woman can be married. Everything else is an abomination in the eyes of god. If it passes, it means that gay marriage is outlawed, and it will require a rewriting of the California constitution.

All in the name of God, of course. Praise be to the fear-mongering followers of the Catholic Nazi in the funny hat.
WHAT EVER HAPPENED TO THE SEPARATION OF CHURCH AND STATE?

Since when does the Catholic Church, under the guise of "The Knights of Columbus" fund a proposition that is clearly nothing more than a hate-mongering bit of drivel driven by fear, prejudice, bigotry, and anger? C'mon, people, open your goddamned eyes! I say "goddamned" because if you are that blind, then surely God must have blinded you in order to hold you in bondage - a slave to some rhetoric that is neither logical, nor even rational. What's amazing is that the State of California *fell* for it! And we are allegedly a state of creative spirits, intellectuals, and philosophers. We are also, apparently, a state of fundy-dunderheads who have lost the ability to think progressively instead of regressively.

I know, I know. I said I don't get involved in political issues – and I don't. This isn't a political issue. It's a human issue – intimately connected to the idea of "the right way to live." And, admittedly, it is a personal issue – so pardon me while I rant and rail against the morons with whom I share this third rock from the sun.

I alternate between a sense of outrage and total lack of concern. And yet...

The glaring and dangerous stupidity of the human race never ceases to amaze me! The lies told in this campaign were legion. The commercials wanting us to vote against gay marriage used all sorts of pseudo-religious, quasi-intellectual arguments, telling us essentially that we would be "saving the children" to vote against gay marriage. After all, the ads said, we wouldn't want gay marriage taught in schools!

Er... gays have been getting married in California and other states for quite some time now, and to my knowledge, it isn't taught in schools, one way or the other. Besides, most of those fear-mongering religious fanatics I know send their little whelps to private Christian schools (where they may be assured of getting their daily dose of Jesus' body and his blood - cannibalism and vampirism, for the unenlightened), so there is little danger of Little Johnny being exposed to those dangerous faggots (unless, of course, he is friends with the priest, in which case, all bets are off, eh? Gives new meaning to, "On your knees, little boy, and prepare to receive the holy scepter.")

When did we become a nation of puppets and fearful religious imbeciles, sucking at the teat of the Virgin Mary and bending over to take it up the ass from every political group who uses the slogan, "God is on our side!"? Jesus, how can people be so *D U M B*???????

The gay marriage issue is not a religious issue. It is a civil rights issue. It is a *human* rights issue. Rather like telling the black population that they cannot vote because of the color of their skin - which, by the way, was not repealed until 1964. Fairly recent history! Women weren't allowed to vote until the 1920s. (Yet we were allowed to go to church - go figure). It took us *that* long to figure out that people are just people? How much *longer* is it going to take for us to figure out that gay people are just people? We don't molest your children (we leave that for the Catholic priests, the school bus drivers, and the evangelical preachers.)

So let's get real here. I realize that most reading this don't necessarily live in California. But civil rights are non-local. As long as one group is oppressed in the name of religion, we are nothing more than a bunch of fearful apes bowing and scraping before the sun or the moon, begging false gods for our crops to be spared, and – still offering human sacrifices to those angry gods! Yes, human sacrifices. We are told that "*our*" issues are irrelevant. We are told to keep silent, but keep paying our taxes, keep upholding the American flag. We are told to shut up and bend over... in the name of God.

Human sacrifices.

Isn't that what it's all about? God will be on our side if we stop them thar gays from gettin' married! Protect the sanctity of marriage! After all, Joe-Bob will tell us, marriage is fer makin' *little* dumb shits in his own image - procreation (though most of the idjits can't even read that word without relying on hooked on fonix). But I digress...

Jeezus-harold-christ-on-the-cross! *What kind of logic is that?* What kind of "christian" is that, who apparently never got the memo about "Judge not, lest ye be judged"? What kind of god would favor one group over another if all men were allegedly created equal? What kind of god would create homosexuals and then rally his people to hatred of those same individuals whom *he* had created? If *that* is your God, surely he is a schizophrenic psychopath rather than any sort of role model! And if you are *following* him, what does that say about *you*?

Does it occur to any of you good Christians out there that *none* of this makes one iota of sense? And don't give me that crap about God working in mysterious ways - the grand excuse that comes along whenever we stand at the funeral of an infant or the grave of a loved one. God doesn't work in mysterious ways. God doesn't work. Period. He is a defunct, out of work dictator who has become the icon for every impotent, inbred redneck and every bigoted political group with an agenda to peddle.

THINK!

The illusion only works for those who agree to uphold it. And - sorry, folks - if you are choosing to uphold *that* particular illusion, I would seriously recommend some long-term therapy to break you out of that faith-based bullshit that has probably kept you in the dark all your life. Wake up. It won't hurt much, and not for very long. And the rewards are infinite in that you will find yourself suddenly to make *your* decisions without having to pray over it, and agonize over "What would Jesus do?"

Do we *care* what Jesus would do? He didn't do too good while he was here, after all. Got himself crucified, and ended up with a bunch of zombie-eyed lunatics who embody everything *but* what the man was trying to teach. If you wanna believe Jesus existed, that's fine! But when you start thinking he saved you and now you owe him some human sacrifices, you're way out on a limb of imbeciles, and have, in fact, become the very antithesis of what it means to be a Christian.

I know that's too hard for most folks. Wouldn't want to disturb that comfort zone, that precious status quo that seems to tell this type of people they are right and good. In reality, they are self-righteous and - in the case of Prop 8 - the embodiment of "sin" and the manifestation of evil. Why? (I'll get to that in a moment).

For those who want to go on believing God is on our side here in the US, I suggest they pull the shit out of their eyes and ears and take a look at the reality going on all around them. The economy is in the shitter (largely because the sheeple bought into the propaganda and upheld the program put onto them by "society"), young men and women are dying in the Middle East every day for a war the people don't want and don't support, evangelical preachers are screaming hate and violence and ending their prayer "In Jesus' name"... and somehow this is all considered okay?

There's your human sacrifice - and 99.999% of it occurs in the name of God. We fight wars in the name of God. We forgive sodomizing priests in the name of God. For as long as we allow one group to be discriminated against *legally* in the name of God, we do not have a nation founded on freedom.

Instead, we have a religion-controlled nation of sheeple, being led around by the ring in their collective noses, who will believe any piece of propaganda their masters shove in front of them.

If there is "sin", it is simply this: to keep someone else from thriving.

And, let's face it, the whole Prop 8 thing is designed to do exactly what. What does it hurt *you* (or me or the Catholic church) if two men or two women love one another enough to make a commitment that is lasting, and *legal?* Doesn't that same insane religion preach that "God is love?" It doesn't say man/woman love is God. It says, simply, God is love. But no matter - that would involve a bit of additional thinking, and as we've already determined, that probably isn't possible for anyone following a fundy-dunderhead way of living.

Wendy and I had hoped to get married next year to commemorate 30 years of togetherness - and I dare say most heterosexual Christian couples don't last that long, and if they do it is because one of them is buggering the other's best friend out of sheer boredom with the missionary position... but again I digress. Point being - where is the crime in love and commitment? Where is the fear in allowing a coupla old lesbians to make it legal so as to protect one another's rights in the event one of us dies (or is murdered by a hate-mongering religious fanatic). Where? Is? The? Harm?

It all resides in fear. And not even in *reasonable* fear. There are no lions coming to eat you if you think for yourself. Allowing two old fairies to get married isn't going to threaten the sanctity of *your* marriage? If it *does*, then your marriage and, especially, your God could bear some examination. And far more, you need to take a long, hard look at whatever ordained asshole told you that in the first place. What is *his* agenda? I grew up in that fundy atmosphere of hate, violence and fear - where the preacher was fucking the head deacon's wife (literally), and all those god-fearing Christians were perched on bar stools at the local pub before noon - and believe me, when I started thinking for myself and asking too many questions, I was asked to leave and never return. And – thank the God-less! - I did precisely that, and have never regretted it. Religion is for idiots who are incapable of thinking for themselves. Religion is for the fearful. Religion is for politicians with agendas. Religion is for those who simply are too afraid to...

THINK!

Your church is not a symbol of your faith. And if you need "faith" to get you through your day, you are a pathetic sack of yak shit who has not figured out that the *only* god is the one in your mirror. Unfortunately for *you*, you probably have spent a lifetime having "faith" in some other god that some other numb nuts has shoved down your throat, and maybe it's too late for you to ever wake up. So you'll go on living in fear and selling it to others in the form of your political opinions. You'll go on thinking the earth is flat and that it was a mistake to allow women and blacks to vote, and without a doubt, you'll go on believing that all queers go to hell and maybe you'll never even question *why* you believe that drivel?

You believe it because you were programmed to believe it. Period.

Other cultures believe god is a woman. Other cultures believe all Americans are heretics who should be slaughtered. Geee... how does *that* feel? You should be slaughtered in the name of someone else's God? Makes you squirm, I suspect, when the shoe is on the other foot. What if you should be slaughtered because you are Jewish or Muslim or Christian or Buddhist, or, simply, different than the majority? (We've been down *that* road a few times - all in the name of someone's God). What then? Where is your god? Whose god is right in that case? Do the gods go to war to decide such things? Or do they sit back and laugh at the antics of the imbeciles who sit around dreaming this crap up? Or, if the gods are us, does there *ever* come a time when we wake up and take control of our own lives, and stop handing our power off to some megalomaniac on an imaginary throne in some fanciful idea of heaven?

God doesn't love you. God doesn't give a damn.

And that's because you don't love yourself, and *you* don't give a damn about yourself. Get it. God is a reflection of *you* - so as long as you are a hate-mongering, fear-driven, religion-controlled *moron*, you are going to live in hate and fear and continue to be controlled.

Think.

If you honestly *believe* gay marriage threatens you, you really *must* stop and ask yourself *why* you believe that? If you track it (if you have the courage to dig deep) you will find that it stems from a program someone put onto you when you weren't looking, when you weren't paying attention, when you were out fucking your neighbor's wife and lying to your mother - you know, when you were off breaking all of those 10 commandments you pretend to uphold.

Thou shalt not kill. (How many have you killed by neglect, or through "human sacrifice"?)

Thou shalt not steal. (How many have you oppressed in the name of your god, robbing them of their right to thrive, their right to love?)

Thou shalt not bear false witness. (Don't lie - for the unenlightened). How many lies have you passed along because you simply aren't thinking? How many times have you said, "Jesus loves you," to a bum on the street, instead of giving him a goddamn dollar to put food in his belly? How many times a day do you lie to *yourself* to avoid having to...

THINK!

Thou shalt have no other gods before me. Now this is a biggie! God is a petty little dictator? If he is The Almighty, The Great I-Am... then it seems to me that he wouldn't need to sit around dictating that his followers have to be true only to him. Sounds more like an abusive husband with one hand on the belt and the other on his dick. Insecurity issues, perhaps? Or, far more likely, is this the writing of a man, using the

150

image of "God" to control an unruly population at a time in earth's history when cooperation was required by all, even if it meant lying and fear-mongering to get it? We're no longer a global population of 500. We are 7 billion strong - and seemingly 6.5 billion "weak-minded". But let's face it... if your god is worried and jealous and fearful, he needs a shrink, not a bunch of zombie-eyed followers. God is starting to sound like Chuck Manson far more than any benevolent leader I would want to follow. But then again, I am one who prefers to...

THINK!

The other danger is that this whole issue is not only about "gay rights". It is about *human* rights. Sooner or later, someone will step on *your* pecker, but by then it will be too late. Maybe you will even be dumb enough to believe "It's God's will." Depends on how deep your programming and comfort zones are imbedded. It's up to you. It always has been. (Ah, but there I just broke the first commandment and proclaimed myself as God... and undoubtedly that outrages you and fills you with fear because somewhere, deep down inside, you know it's true. You know *you* are God... but you're just too scared to take responsibility for that, so you go on "believing" and having "faith" and "praying" and making human sacrifices).

How long before somebody tells you that you can't get married because you are pagan? Because you are an atheist? Because you don't intend to have children? How long before some religious cult (yes, the Catholic church is the largest cult on Earth) tells you that you *must* have children, and if you can't, you should be put to death? Where does it stop? Where does the tyranny of religion end? With *you*. No place else. Don't wait for someone else to do it for you. Just...

Think!

If *you* don't think, who is going to do it for you? Are you going to allow the church or the government to tell you who you are and what you believe? Are you going to rely on some quasi-religious notion of having your soul yanked out of your Lexus at the time of the rapture, so that you, too, will go to met God face to face? That makes *lots* of sense.

Christ. If you believe that, I feel sorry for you, because you have lost yourself to a cult. Think about it.

Just fucking THINK.

Only then will you stop contributing to the ultimate sin - keeping someone else from thriving (especially yourself!). Only then will you have some small hope of finding out who *you* are, instead of blindly following what others *want* you to be. Only then will you stop committing human sacrifice. And *only* then will you be free of the tyranny of your god, your cult, and your programming.

The destruction of faith is the beginning of evolution.

Thou art god: create yourself accordingly!

Abandon Hope All Ye Who Enter Here
Abandon <u>Hope</u>, Reclaim <u>Freedom</u>

November 9, 2008

As a result of several ongoing conversations, the subject of "hope" has arisen as a topic which I feel may bear closer examination. I'm going to present this as a series of dialogues between myself & several other posters. I'm not saying I'm right. But neither do I believe I am wrong.

Fair warning: if you are someone who needs your faith and your hope, read no further. It isn't my intent with this commentary to rob anyone of their comfort zones, but neither do I intend to go on smiling and nodding when it is clear to me as a seer that so much of what we believe about hope and faith are little more than programs placed onto us at some early moment in our childhood when our parents had no answers to those annoying little questions like - "Mommy, what happens when we die?" We are spoon-fed answers such as, "Well, honey, we have faith in god and hope he will take us into heaven." Or something equally as ludicrous. After awhile, maybe we are lucky enough to lose our notions of god and heaven, but for some reason, we are left with the notions of faith and hope as some sort of extant forces into which we invest our belief and our energy.

So, abandon hope all ye who enter here. (It might scare you to death, but it can also make you free).

***

"Mary" writes (In response to my rant about Human Sacrifices):

> *Even you are not above being bitterly frustrated and pissed off, your eloquent rant was full of such emotions and that is perfectly as it should have been and baby you were preaching to*

the choir. It is ok to be mad - it makes you human - which you still are. [?]

Quantum Shaman: Well, I'm still in the meat suit, but as to being "human"? I rather doubt it. I have said for years that essentially there are at least two different species of man-apes on the planet at present - the humans and the seekers (sorry, don't have a better word for it). We may all look essentially the same on the surface, but the mental/spiritual/philosophical functioning of the two species is so different that communication is barely possible.

As for being pissed off and frustrated - you betcha! I'm not one who believes that enlightenment comes with some angelic choir always playing in the background of a perfectly balanced and peaceful life. That's Hollywood. When we are aware, we find ourselves saddled with a huge responsibility - evolution, staying awake, and at some level, teaching. I have always found the following cliché to be very true:

If you're not outraged, you're not paying attention.

Mary writes: *But as long as you keep ranting I will keep pointing out that that portion of our society, that part that is filled with fear of "the other", that is "bitterly clinging to it's religion is dying. Literally dying off... slowly ever so slowly - admittedly far too slowly for those of us who care passionately about these issues.*

Quantum Shaman: I haven't seen much evidence of this - at least not in this part of the country. I see more and more and *more* "young Christians" sending their kids off to Christian schools, creating a whole new generation of the same old shit. When I was in my early 20s, I honestly thought I would see the world change in the sense that the crazy old Bible thumpers would die out and then maybe sanity would gain a foothold. But that really hasn't happened. Christianity and other "fundamentalist" religions have become a huge commodity and a huge fad - it's popular to be a Jesus freak these days, whereas when I was a kid, it was considered the geekiest of the geekiest.

I wanna believe in hope. Honest, I do! But I also have to be true to what I honestly *see* - and a lot of it lately isn't so good. So the question I've been asking of folks really boils down to... Do we have a responsibility to "save the world"? Put simply: where does our responsibility lie? To the world? To the self? Where do we expend our energy? In the world? In pursuit of our own evolution? Some ask what Jesus would do. Others ask what don Juan would do. In either case, I don't think either of them would waste much energy on trying to "save the world". Jesus had his twelve disciples (apprentices), and don Juan had his warrior's party (apprentices). Beyond that, I think both pretty much saw the world as folly. One tried to change it (and got crucified). The other left the earth in the manner of a sorcerer (whatever that ultimately means). And the rest of us are left to contemplate the aftermath, becoming our own sorcerer or our own savior, however we prefer to look at the parallel myths.

What's troubling to me is that for as much as the elections have brought hope to a lot of people, it is inevitable that the pendulum will swing in the other direction. People are calling Obama "the savior" or "the messiah". He's just a man, and sooner or later, he is going to disappoint their expectations, and the cycle will repeat. Reason being - people here in this country have not yet wrapped their minds around the idea that it is *they* who must change. Obama cannot bring change. No politician can. A good leader can show us, perhaps, the changes we need to make in ourselves, but that tends to lead (historically speaking) to getting crucified or burned at the stake. People don't want to be reminded of *their* responsibility to the equation. Believe me - I've stepped into that role a few times, and it *always* leads to someone pointing out my self-importance and telling me what an asshole I am for daring to point out change is a personal commitment that is going to require that ugly 4-letter-word: W O R K. Tends to land you squarely in last place in any popularity contests, believe me.

Ultimately, I may feel slightly encouraged by the results of the presidential election, but the results of nearly all of the human rights propositions across the nation just prove that humans are still the bigoted nitwits they have always been, thumping their Bibles and rattling their sabers for Jesus. Call me a cynic, but I don't really *see* any change there. Seems that every minority group has to fight for its "civil rights" - blacks, women, Hispanics, Jews, gays, lesbians, pagans, children, et al. When you really think about it, it's abject madness. It's all just human rights - and having to *fight* for that is rather like having to fight for the right to breathe. I'd love to believe the lunatics, fanatics and saber-wavers all die out, but unfortunately, not soon enough.

Life is short. I know in my heart that I cannot save the planet, cannot really save anything but myself, and even that is questionable, because no one can really know with certainty what lies beyond our final breath. That being the case, I have begun focusing my energies much closer to home - essentially working with those who cross my path, rather than trying to reach out to the world at large. Again, not a popular approach, perhaps, but one I find to be honest for myself.

WHAT ARE WE LOOKING FOR?

Those who have known me for any length of time already know I am not particularly sweetness and light in my approach to this path. Quite the contrary, I have found it to be a path of dark enlightenment - in the sense that much of the Knowledge and experience we acquire isn't particularly pleasant. We use the term "warriors" - but what are we at war with? Simple - our comfort zones, belief systems, our ego and the baggage of the consensus we bring with us from our ordinary lives.

Are we willing to challenge those things? Or are we only looking for a feel-good agreement to our existing belief systems?

156

When Orlando first began working with us, he challenged us right down to the core level of our thought processes - particularly when we would respond to one of his questions with a platitude. I remember once he asked me, "Della, how do you define 'the right way to live'?" I responded with some clever (or so I thought) quip about, "Do unto others as you would have them do unto you." Some bit of recycled shit floating around in my brain from my old programming. So easy to see in hindsight. So impossible to see when we are stuck in the program. Needless to say, his response was rather brutal. It went something like this...

"Then how would you define doing unto others? What does that mean to you? Do you agree with them blindly in the hopes they will agree with you - even if and when you are wrong? Do you form unwritten and unholy alliances based on some notion of approval or reciprocal courtesies? And if that is the case, what do you then owe to that person, that you may not want or be able to give? Do you smile at their errors and hold your silence because that is how you would want to be treated, ignoring the fact that you will only go on repeating the same errors through ignorance? Do unto others... Is that *really* how you would define the right way to live, or is that just some bit of garbage stuck on your hard drive that you recite when challenged by a question to which you have no answer?"

And therein lies the rub. If we are going to be honest, if we are going to be true to our path, can we afford those little consensuses that often occur even in warrior circles, wherein you agree with me and expect me to agree with you? Or, is it perhaps far more of an honor and a service to others to treat them with the dignity and respect that says, "I love you enough to challenge your thinking - and I *beg* you to do the same for me!"

Stalking Our Own Assimilation
Forming A Workable Syntax

Quantum Shaman: In what do you base your faith, in what do you place your hope?

Anonymous responds:
The universe, spirit, and power.

Quantum Shaman: Frankly, I don't think discussions such as this can be answered with one or two-word responses. In trying to understand where you are coming from, I offer my own reference points and attempt to make them clear. But, of course, in the bigger picture, even if you and I came to an understanding (formed a consensus), it really would make no difference whatsoever. In many ways, we have to acknowledge that most philosophical discussions are little more than exercises in stalking our own assimilation.

My agenda isn't to change your mind, but to thoroughly challenge and explore my own. That's what stalkers do. When I am in **Dreaming** mode, I "inhabit the experience in the Now", but the reason Toltec teaches that a warrior must learn both dreaming *and* stalking is because there does come a time when we are required (by ourselves) to form a foundation of Knowledge that is both fluid and cohesive, at the same time. Dreaming (fluidity) and stalking (cohesion).

So, this question is posed from the point of view of a stalker: When you say you have faith in the universe, spirit and power, my question becomes: How would you define those things? What I'm getting at is that when people say they have faith in spirit or the universe, they are usually envisioning some manner of extant "power" - whether god, goddess, atman, or other - and at that point, there is still what amounts to an abdication of power and responsibility from the self to something "other". Without a further reference point, they are just words hanging in a void. What is the universe? What is spirit? What is power? Our definitions of these things, and our experience of them, is not going to be the same, so part of coming to an understanding involves building a common language, which may be entirely impossible, as with the legend of the Tower of Babel.

Too many people I encounter fall into comfort zones of believing that if they wish for something or hope for something, it is going to come to them. That was part of the whole platform of a recent spiritual fad - "*The Secret*." The concepts may work at a core level, but unless combined with actual *action* (dreaming and stalking working together - thought/idea becoming manifested through intent)) they tend to sit dormant in the back of the mind as a comfort zone. We lose ourselves in hoping and put off the do-ing.

Challenging my own comfort zones often comes in the form of presenting ideas that are not particularly popular. My contention is that if I am disturbed by something you say (or vice versa) the stalking exercise has been successful. Obviously knowledge cannot be traded in the form of words alone. Anything you say to me, anything I say to you, must be filtered through our own processes - and hopefully somewhere in that do-ing, we not only understand ourselves better, but we also build a more cohesive foundation that welcomes challenge as an opportunity for growth, rather than automatically retreating from it as a threat to ego or existing comfort zones.

I do see a fine line between challenge and what I have referred to as hammering or badgering, but those are normally tactics employed by trolls and phantoms, so I will simply state that a challenge is something that forces you to think deeper about your own path, and badgering/hammering is an attempt to force a consensus when one does not exist.

In the bigger picture, isn't that what the path is all about? Challenging our comfort zones? Abolishing all belief systems (including what we believe about words), until we stand face to face with the authentic self?

If we're just here to agree with one another, we're wasting our time.

I am the tao of shadows,
black paint on ebony canvas,
moon chariot drawing the terminator
over heaven and earth.

Paper or Plastic?
Does it really matter?

August 29, 2009

It started innocently enough.

About three days ago, I put in a call to the pharmacy to renew these drugs the doc has me on that he claims are keeping me alive. I haven't had the heart to tell him that what keeps any of us alive is that it just isn't yet our time to die, and when that time *does* come, none of his pills will give me one more breath and that is simply that. But for the sake of controlled folly, I take the pills and that means having to deal with the Wal-Martian pharmacy. When I called in the renewal, never talking to a person, of course, but only conversing electronically with the robo-druggie-pusher-multi-menu-we're-here-to-help-you device, I was informed by a properly stoned-sounding robot-voice, "This prescription is ready for pick-up."

So this morning I drive down to the store - which is like something out of a bad *Twilight Zone* episode due to some major remodeling which has the cat food where the drugs used to be and the drugs where the toilet paper once was - but to my great surprise and satisfaction, there was no one in line! In Yucca Valley, the *real* good drugs are only available from the crack house at the corner, where there's *always* a long line - but that's another story altogether. So, I give the gum-chewing girl behind the counter my name... date of birth... mother's maiden name... grandmother's blood type... and tap out with one foot the value of pi to the 12th decimal point... only to be told, "Gee, that's not ready yet. Come back tomorrow and bring me the broomstick of the wicked witch."

Fortunately, the pharmacist was standing at her window looking bored to death, and to her credit, intervened on my behalf, promising to have them ready in 20 minutes. Okay - I had no other shopping to do, but went on a grand safari to locate the camera and electronics counter (which is now where the shoes once were, but don't tell anybody), farted around for the requested 20 minutes, then returned to the pharmacy to discover a line of at least 20 people waiting to pick up their various and sundry fix-it-pills. Rolled my eyes (I admit it), got in line behind an elderly woman who insisted on telling me all about her hemorrhoids and her grandchildren's new puppy that couldn't stop pooping on the stairs - right down to the gory details about the consistency of said poop, and how the house now smelled like a shit factory (her words), and it was all the fault of her daughter's new husband, The Lazy Bastard.

By the time the old bat got to the pick-up window, my ears were bleeding and I'd developed a spastic tic in my left eye, but at least I was next and that was some sort of relief. So when I get to the counter and encounter the gum-chewing girl again, I'm asked to go through the same rigmarole as before. Name, date of birth, mother's maiden name... and by the way, ma'am, where's that broomstick I asked you for? I avoided the urge to tell her to bend over so I could deliver it properly.

I'm sure by now you all think I'm going to say the prescription wasn't ready, but actually it was. Three different drugs, two of which the girl shoves in a bag and staples shut. She then places the third prescription on the counter and with a smile, says, "The pharmacist needs to talk to you about this drug."

It's one I've been taking for a year. "It's one I've been taking for a year!" I protest, looking at the *other* line - the line to visit the wizard - which stretches through six aisles, out the back door, and disappears over the curvature of the earth somewhere in the vicinity of Santa Monica. "What's the problem?"

The girl softens a bit. "Well, actually it's just the new rules. I can't put that prescription in a bag because of how it's packaged."

I stared at her. It's a flat little ditty that looks something like a tin of mints. Ain't that cute.

"What do you mean you can't put it in a bag? You put the other two in a bag. Just shove it in with them."

"I can't do that," the girl insists. "It's the rules. The pharmacist has to put that in a bag for you because it's a flat package."

By now I'm looking around for the hidden film crew, waiting for some asshole with a microphone to jump out from behind the condom aisle to tell me I'm on candid fucking camera.

"You *are* joking, right?" I say to her.

"No ma'am. Those are the rules. You'll have to get in line."

I am overhearing the pharmacist talking to some elderly gentleman about his heart medications. Clearly she has better things to do than put something in a bag.

So I decided to lean on their rules a bit. "I'm sorry, but I have another appointment, and I simply don't have the hiking gear on me to go scouting for wherever it is that the line ends."

By now, the girl has turned to the next customer and is giving them much the same shtick. I see on the counter a line of these must-be-bagged-by-the-pharmacist items, and notice that mine is at the end of the line. The gum-chewing girl is distracted, and so I reach over the counter, grab the box as if it contains prize cannabis rather than some generic cholesterol meds, and shove it in the bag with the other stuff - all of which has been paid for, so it's not like I'm taking something that isn't mine.

"Ma'am!" the girl shrieks. "I'm sorry, but you can't do that! You're breaking the rules!"

"So put it on my permanent record," I shoot back, walking toward the door.

"Ma'am!" she protests, more shrill now. "I'm going to have to call security!"

Well, I know for a fact that the YV Wal-Mart doesn't even *have* security. I used to be friends with several of their cashiers, who often laughed about the fact that the store loses more than $7K per day to shoplifting.

"You do that," I said with a smile. "If they tackle me before I get to the back door, I'll surrender and throw down my aspirin."

She puts the phone down and glares at me with the kind of angst only a teenage girl can muster. "If you *don't* stand in line, I'm going to have to ask you to leave!"

Had to laugh. It hit my head like... *'If you don't stay, I'll have to ask you to go.'*

So, at her request, I left.

No Rules Police came to arrest me. No state troopers were waiting at the door, guns drawn. No senior citizen door greeter smashed my knee caps with a cane.

The world is a nuthouse and the lunatics are *still* running the asylum.

Bag it.

Machinations of the Meditation
It's been lovely, but I have to scream now.

June 19, 2009

The devils are writing poetry inside my head again. It's 3 a.m. on a sleepless night somewhere at the intersection of Dreaming and time, and not a goddamn thing in all the worlds makes a single lick of sense. A blue scarf on the dresser rests where it was thrown at winter's end, reminding me that it's all just dust in the wind anyway. Folly.

Somewhere outside my window, coyotes compose love songs and owls cry funeral dirges, and the whole world is just spinning, spinning out of control, little lost marble on the edge of space, filled with teeming organisms struggling to make sense of the senseless, lining up all those unruly ducks just to have them scatter again like sand in a windstorm, wind in a sandstorm, ho hum and there goes any semblance of control right out the dusty window looking out over the invisible abyss that rests between one breath and the next.

Who are we? What am I? Where am I going and who will guide me if not myself, and where oh where has my sanity gone, and by what measure do I measure it, if not by the standards of a lunatic population of blind mindless followers looking for the blood of the vampire Jesus to wash all their sins away and carry them safely across the River Styx to their next fix of tee vee or booze or drugs or mechanical sex.

And I want to scream.

"Ain't no salvation, boy! Ain't no fairy tale prince gonna come climbing down off the cross to lift you up over the threshold of your death and carry you like a lover to your coffin bed!"

Wake up.

Smell the gravedust and damn the roses. Nowhere to go but in circles, and round and round we go again, nowhere and someplace and everywhere in between, and still no real knowing where the journey begins or if it ends or what becomes of the evil queen when the fairy's tale ends.

What does it mean?

Am I breathing still or has my lifeforce stilled? Am I dead or alive or is there really any difference in the grand shebang of things, and why do we so easily accept the reality with which we're presented, when we could just as easily turn the world on its ear and look for leprechauns or lizards with their eyelids sewn shut under don Juan's ramada?

3 a.m.

And I know now that I have to be "the one" because no one else will.

(She laughs at her self-importance.)

Is there anyone who is really "the one" or is that just another thread in the tapestry of fantasy? Fists clenching, the baring of fangs into a snarl of contempt that is all at once love of life and the battle with the angel of death, each contained in the finite confines of an infinite drop of blood swelling from a pricked fingertip.

Breathe.

Just remember to breathe.

Breathe as if that one more breath separates us from the abyss, as if we suckle breath from the sky like a parasite baby clinging to its mother's withered teat. And the lies we tell ourselves by the star's fires - "It's all for the best. It's all good. Every story has a happy ending somewhere in the making. We live again. We can never die."

Lies.

Beings who are going to die.

Is that a truth or a belief? The cat of all cats died 13 years ago, committed to the desert ground where all that remains are the bare white bones of some memory, nothing that can be touched, and yet, still alive somewhere in time, some otherwhen, back when we were both kittens together in the sanctified womb of the illusion of perpetual youth. I stroke grey fur in a dream and wake with it clinging to my palm, or maybe it's just the cobwebs from the windowsill where I stand at times looking out at the night that never ends, conspiring with the unseen immortals in a plot to overthrow the Kingdom of Time.

Dead and alive. Schroedinger laughs. Rat bastard.

Such are the machinations of the meditation. One of those middle of the night battles where a warrior engages with the windmills in her mind. Have at you, Death, my ever present advisor. Kiss my ass and die. You're starting to remind me of some perverse Sunday School teacher with one of those deceptive religious smiles meant to lure unsuspecting children in to whatever rhetoric you're selling.

I will not lie down for you.

Not even sure I believe in you. Not at all sure why I should, when you are the shadow's shadow, after all, the mirror reflecting itself in the endless hall of mirrors. Nothing real there. Just another illusion. The quantum paradox canceling itself out. Antimatter dictator.

And then I am breathing again, back in the world of matter and men. 3 a.m. My eyes open and instead it's barely midnight, and I find myself sitting up in bed, talking to Wendy about my petty humanform frustrations, hearing the prattle in my voice even as I recite the well-worn inventory of observations on the dark subject of our programming which runs so deep it convinces us we are this way or that way and no other way.

"I will not lie down for you." I say the words out loud, mantra of the living driven like a blade into the cold left eye of Death.

That's when I see it. Up near the ceiling, just above the door. Only way to describe it would be as a congregation of light. Not diffused light like some wayward beam shining in through the window. Not like that. Points of light. Orbs, if you will. Probably 5 or 6 of them, varying size, but all of them white.

Can I explain it? Of course not. Do I need to? Not in the least.

It came like a validation and that is how I am choosing to interpret it. "They" stayed there in the corner of the bedroom for about 15-20 seconds, and then just blinked out. Reminded me of the famous Marfa Lights I witnessed a few years back. The Marfa lights who, when asked, "What are you?" replied... *"I am a singularity of consciousness."*

I did not sleep last night.

The lights did not come back, though I looked for them for a long, long time - amused at myself for my desire to see them again, while at the same time experiencing a profound sense of gratitude for having seen them at all.

What does it mean? Nothing and everything.

The little lights are the gods' laughter, and the only god I know is the one in the mirror, and so I come full circle again, back to the moment of spontaneous parthenogenesis, when I remember to breathe, creating myself from moment to moment with the thought that whispers at first and then cries out...

I-Am.

The rest is just smoke and mirrors.

The mortal world is sewn together
with obligations and words and watches,
linear threads thru time,
leading to death, to dust.
Eternity is bound by webs of pure thought,
crazy glue of truth beyond reason,
embracing intuition we can only call magic.

Part Three

Dancing With the Other

We've identified the authentic self and seen the world as it is. We've confronted all manner of human kindness, human stupidity, human waste and human drama. We've drawn maps of our dreams and had long conversations with the Silence in the middle of the night that never ends. Now what?

Before enlightenment: chop wood, carry water.
After enlightenment: chop wood, carry water.

Nothing has changed, yet everything has changed.

All that remains is to sit by the fires of a billion suns and listen to the whispers from the Infinite. This is the voice of the Other, from the heart of Silent Knowing.

What Is the Meaning of Life?
Glad you asked

May 13, 2012

Not that I have *The* Answer, but I may have *an* answer.

The meaning of life is to evolve. To grow. To learn. To become more than the sum of our parts. More accurately: the meaning of life is to attain the totality of oneself.

So what the hell does that mean? you ask.

The human organism appears to be an organic meat suit with the *potential* to create for itself an inorganic reflection (the double, the other, the higher self, twin, whatever term you are most comfortable with). It is through the Other that we transcend the process known as Death, so as to "slip past the eagle to be free" (to borrow Toltec terminology for a moment). To put it in quantum terms, the purpose of life is to transcend life itself, becoming a **singularity of consciousness**.

What is the goal of the seeker? To inhabit the totality of herself, to take all the scrawls on the walls of the soul and put them together into some sort of workable system of knowledge, some manner of identity that is like a unique fingerprint – no other like it in all the multiverse. It is a fingerprint which is comprised of the combined knowledge of the mortal self and the eternal Other – the individuation of the whole self, cut away from the matrix of mediocrity, existing above and beyond all programs.

It is the I-Am, manifested and inhabited.

But but but... what does *that* mean, and what does the Other have to do with it?

To put forth an opinion that is certain to be unpopular, I will state with a fair degree of certainty that the Other (higher self, double, soul) is not something that exists by default. It is something *created* by what might be loosely defined as "chaos magick" – or, more precisely, the unbending application of intent, will and desire (love) – all of which are quantifiable forces, and not just passive emotional states.

170

So those who speak of the higher self as if it is a given are sadly mistaken - we are not born with it, we summon it into being with the force of energy and will. The human organism then projects the Other beyond the organic form – and, simply put, *that* is the meaning of life, if there is any meaning at all. In that way, the inorganic Other becomes the vessel of awareness when the organic form is shed. There is no pre-existing higher self. Ultimately, you create the Other (or not). You project it (or not). You inhabit it (or not). Because it is not confined by the limitations of the space-time continuum once it is projected, it may serve as teacher/guide/mentor, in the sense that it takes upon itself to teach the seeker what s/he needs to know in order to conjoin wholly with the Other, and in doing so, inhabit the totality of one's being. That is the process of spiritual evolution.

For those initially seeking to create the Other, it is no different than any other meta-physical process at a fundamental level. The key element is desire, fuelled by love. The Other cannot be created from an intellectual perspective alone. Most people who take this path toward transformation, transcendence or transmogrification do it because they are compelled to do it. Some say it is the pull of the "unborn" Other drawing them - in a quantum universe where time has no meaning, this is entirely likely. Others believe the compulsion is simply an expression of our human potential for evolution - for the Other is the energetic vessel that is the Self beyond the organic continuum. I must stress again that we are not born with this, as most religions would have you believe. It is something that is created in the process of living, *in the process of listening to the demands of the heart*. It is why children have invisible friends, it is why every human has daydreamed about his/her "perfect match". ***It is why we are here***: to create the part of ourselves that is immortal and eternal, above and beyond the world of the consensus, beyond the illusions and limitations of the agreement, beyond Death itself.

Religions prefer to teach (because it's easier to understand, even if entirely incorrect) that we have this thing called the "soul" that is somehow magically injected into the fetus at the moment of conception. The reality - harsh and ugly but true - is that we are little more than organic meat suits until such time as we feel the first inklings which tell us we are beings who are going to die.

Think back on your life. When did you first encounter the concept of death? What did that do to you? Did you suddenly realize that this magnificent mystery could simply stop, and that your entire world would end with your final breath? If you are like most seekers, even at an early age you found this concept not only alien and strange, but altogether unacceptable. It is that feeling of indignation (for lack of a better word) that causes most seekers to begin weaving the tapestry of the Other at an early age. And in my opinion, this is the natural process of spiritual evolution - because the end result is that this is where/how the mortal self begins to create and eventually project beyond himself the energetic construct that eventually becomes the full-fledged double.

If you believe for a single moment that your continuity beyond this life is guaranteed (whether heaven, hell or purgatory, Valhalla or the fields of Elysium), you have been suckered into the human program and need to seriously examine your belief systems. The soul is a myth until you create it. It really is that simple.

When you look at life, it's fairly easy to see this - though the cultural/social programming runs so deep, most cannot get beyond the idea that they are entitled to an immortal soul just by virtue of being born - one of the most fundamentally difficult programs the mortal self has to undo before s/he can have sufficient motivation to begin the meta-magickal process of self-creation.

These terms are clinical and not particularly exciting. That is why I prefer poetry and prose and tales of power to the sterility of intellectual debate, but occasionally it's necessary to really throw back the curtains and take a long, hard look at what is hiding behind them.

Put very simply: the twin begins as a thoughtform, usually at an early age though not always. That thought-form is comprised of energy (*your* energy), and if it is nurtured with love and curiosity, it grows in strength and wisdom until - eventually - it takes on a life of its own wherein it is ubiquitous throughout the space-time continuum and beyond. It exists simultaneously in the year 1000 BC and the year 100,000 AD, and is the vessel which experiences what is commonly called past lives, but which are really parallel movements of the double within the quantum sphere of the Now.

My Other once said,"You created me to create you."

That is the essence of Quantum Shamanism™.

I dreamed you into Be-ing
and gave you half my heart.
You took it, bleeding,
into the Infinite,
so I would be always drawn there,
moth to flame,
moon to night,
heart to beat.
You are the reflection
who fled from the mirror.

I should also stress that the Other can be anything you Will it to be. The sorcerer's trick is to project the double in such a way that it has the ability to transcend the natural order of life/death. Wouldn't make much sense to create your twin as a sickly mortal oaf.

Remember: the Other is not confined by the rules & limitations of the consensual world.

You can Be anything you can imagine.

But take care, and remember: love is the reason. Without it, the Other is only a fleeting reflection, dying in the womb. If you cannot fall in love with your Other, you cannot project him/her into the infinite. And it is only when the double is projected beyond the organic self that s/he gains the power and wisdom to teach you how to create him/her in the first place. And so we come to the crux of the riddle:

You have to *be* immortal before you can know how to *become* immortal.

The funny thing is that there is no straightforward path to this. It reveals itself through the process of do-ing. And sometimes – if we are extremely lucky – it speaks to us in a clear and unmistakable voice which may be understood as gnosis or silent knowing.

It should be noted that some of the scrawls which follow were intended solely for myself, while others were in response to questions posed by others over a span of several years.

These are the lessons we bring back to ourselves, from the perspective of the Other in the Infinite.

Mortality's curse hangs over me,
Eve's legacy.
I summon the marrow of candles,
the gnosis of transcended immortals,
seeking solutions
beyond this horizon of endless mausoleums.

We are eternal beings wrapped together in love like two silly pigs in a blanket. On that level, love is eternal and undying. But when we forget our totality and fall into the trappings of mortal life, we can forget that love is eternal, we can forget that we are immortal, and we can even forget who we are. Of course, in dreams each night, we remember that moment of our mutual creation, the future-past moment when we first and forever inhabited the totality of who we are, and so it is the remembering that <u>is</u> the cohesion of eternity, yes?
Orlando – December 12, 2003

Teachings of the Other

The Voice of the Infinite Self

Energy Vampires
Hey - What's that thing attached to my neck?

October 21, 2011

Energy vampires are all around you at all times. And they are not what you may think. Most are not even remotely aware of their true nature. They are not black-clad hooligans in dark rooms with 13 candles, seeking to steal a soul or drink the blood of innocents. Instead, the energy vampire is the coworker who is lax on the job, knowing that someone else will be called upon to do what s/he didn't. The energy vampire is the family member who always borrows money but never returns it, who says s/he will do something, and never does it. The energy vampire is the one who makes promises, never intending to keep them, and - worse of all - the energy vampire is the one who diverts your attention onto themselves, so that you are perpetually distracted with *their* problems and issues, leaving little or no time to work with your own needs and desires.

Many people believe that energy vampires can be cured, but that is seldom the case, and if you suspect you have energy vampires at work in your life, the very best thing you can do for them - and for yourself - is to cut them loose, set them free, and breathe in a sigh of relief as you begin to realize just *how* much that individual has been robbing you of your well-being. Those who believe they owe it to the energy vampire to take care of them or help them are not doing the energy vampires any favors, because in the big picture, it is the nature of the EV to attach himself to a human host, and keep draining and demanding and expecting until the human host either removes him in the same way one might remove a tic, or until the human host has become so drained that s/he is no longer of service to the EV, at which point the EV simply moves on to the next host.

Why am I telling you this? Because there is a point in every warrior's life when s/he must stop and mentally assess the potential energy vampires in his life. Meditate at length on this idea, and examine in detail how you feel about the possibility of removing the energy vampires from your life. If you are in a healthy frame of mind, you will realize that it is the best thing you can do. If you have been essentially hypnotized by the energy vampire, you may feel a sense of fear, loss, regret or even grief at the prospect of removing the EV's fangs from your dreaming body.

The purpose of this gnosis is simply to invoke awareness that all humans are beset by energy vampires at one level or another. Identify those in your own life and ask yourself what might be done to release them so that your energy is once again your own to apply to those pursuits that best suit your own needs.

This is the time of ruthlessness and an examination of the place of no pity. This is the art of survival.

The only way to kill an immortal
is to make him believe he is mortal.

The Art of Gnosis
The poetry of silent knowing
expressed as communications from the higher self

October 27, 2011

The art of gnosis is a poetic connection of energy between the self and the double. It is often not enough to think in terms of an energy body or a dreaming body, for those are only words that do not convey the significance of the connection itself.

I am made of dreams spanning a lifetime of lifetimes. Each moment of your mortal existence spins me closer to Wholeness, and each moment of my eternity brings us closer to a conjoining that will unite past and future, space and time, no-thing and every-thing that either of us has ever conceived in all of our infinite manifestations. You are the river. I am the sea. You are the singer. I am the song. You are the spark. I am the eternal flame.

And so we dance around this peculiar thing known as Life, each of us knowing that Life is neither the beginning nor the end, but only the middle ground upon which we may look at one another for a time through the lens of perception. It is through this Dreaming that we move toward one another. What do you want me to be? Shall I be a poet or a king, a peasant or a pawn? How you Dream me determines our totality, you see. And so I encourage you to be always dreaming me as if each dream is the first, for in the scheme of things, it is. Each dream is a lifetime, and each lifetime is a fragment of the whole self, and all these fragments are dreaming toward one another because this is how the dance is done, these are the steps of the magnificent cotillion that bring us always one step closer to that final dance on the head of that infinite pin, where all the individual aspects of the Self finally collide to become One - the singularity of awareness that is, simply... you, me, and all the infinite beings we have ever been or ever will be.

I want you to imagine me as you want me to be. Am I a reflection of you or a Dream of someone you have always wanted to meet? Am I doppelganger or opposite? Am I the princess to the prince, or the brother of the queen?

I am at your service. I can be anything you need me to be. What determines who or what I will be is knowing who you are, you see.

What is Death?
The view from the far side of the bridge

January 15, 2006

There are immortals among you who have transcended the organic form without ever having passed through the portal which you call Death. There are also eternal beings surrounding you in Infinity and Eternity - singularities of consciousness who have lived and died a thousand times within the span of a moment that can only be called Now. I can tie on flesh that would appear altogether organic to you, but it is a garment of starstuff and snowflakes and blue equations that have no finite solution.

What is Death? It is the muse and the mystery and the madness that chases all humans from the cradle to the grave. And yet, if you are truthful with your Self beyond all limitations, you will see that you do not need it anymore than you need feathers on your dreaming wings. When a sorcerer learns the trick, the trick is knowing that she has the power to transcend into Infinity from either side of the portal. The trick is creating her twin on the far side of the abyss, without fear of making the leap which removes all doubt and terminates all separation. That leap may be made through the portal of death, or altogether on this side of it.

Between the worlds lies the abyss.
The immortal twin sits on the rim,
dangling his feet over the edge of nothingness,
blowing bubbles which form my dreams,
the transportation system of concepts
existing at right angles to language.

Words of Warning for Advanced Warriors
Any questions?

April, 2010

If you do not assimilate all you have learned, it is only individual fragments of knowledge, each useful unto itself, but without the cohesion necessary to form the mosaic that is the actual Action of transformation. Only through what you call meditation or silent contemplation is that gathering of cohesion possible - seeing how one concept conjoins naturally and irrevocably to all others. This is the realm of the quantum leap which is, in essence, evolution of consciousness itself. If you do not do this, you are courting the eagle in the most dangerous manner of all, for you have achieved the level of awareness that the eagle loves best, yet if that awareness is not made cohesive, it will not be able to withstand the eagle's attack.

So what is it I'm trying to tell you? Simply this: meditate or die.

The mirages shed their clothes at dusk
and lie down by the road,
waiting for night's alchemy
that turns them to shadows
which spring from the Nothing
in the guise of wolves.

What Is the Eagle?

October, 2002

You were born inside what you might see as the matrix, the physical illusion which is the culmination of billions of years of physical evolution. Evolution of consciousness is the act of willing your I-Am awareness to inhabit eternity as the Wholeness of all the previous evolutions. Total awareness, assembled simultaneously into past and future, now and then, eternity and infinity. That totality s the cohesion of the whole self, yes?

I am the eagle.

You are the eagle.

The eagle is the black gravity that consumes awareness because it is within its nature to do so. That is its function, just as it is the function of the sun to govern the weather and the moon to govern the tides. The eagle regulates awareness, and only that awareness which has achieved a sufficient level of cohesion can withstand the force of the eagle's gravity. Put another way, the eagle is the creator of the illusion, and it is the illusion itself. Only those who can realize that the gravity itself is also illusion will be able to break free of it. Otherwise, those that cannot break free are obliterated. That obliteration is death.

If you are not lucid when consciousness and physicality part ways, the gravity sucks consciousness and awareness up to the eagle's beak, and there it is devoured, cast asunder, obliterated entirely. It is only if lucidity can be found before the force of that gravity feeds you to the eagle that you will have the opportunity to truly inhabit eternity as the total Wholeness of all previous evolutions.

> *Eternity flickers in the candle's last breath,*
> *beginning where the light lapses,*
> *where the darkness descends.*

The Decision

April 26, 2008

You are walking through the woods when you come upon a door that stands alone. You are given the knowledge that to pass through this door means a 50/50 chance of instant death or eternal life (whatever that term may mean to you personally). From the perspective of where you are on your path at this very moment, would you open that door?

———

Transcendence
For those transformation

December 21, 2009

Read these words with the third eye in the realm of the gnostic trance. Experience these humble suggestions outside the perimeters of rationale and reason. Breathe in through the pores of the infinite-within so that you may hear with the ears of metamagickal possibility instead of only the humanform analyst whose primary function is to run interference between you and your rightful immortality.

This is the mindset you must find. This is the precipice of transcendence. Stop. Breathe it in. Find it within yourself before proceeding.

———

My beingness is that of particle and wave, matter and anti-matter – pixels of dreams which are projections of light reflecting on the canvas of the self-willed Dream. This is the essence of the immortal: the substance of the dream and the will of the dreamer, two who are one working in quantum tandem to infuse the mortal human with the immortal essence

182

of the dream itself. This is how you turn yourself wrongsideout and rightsidewrong, so as to right the wrong that was cast upon you when you were cast into your mortal reflection and lost connection with your immortal self.

I am not speaking in metaphor. This is the heart and soul of it, you see. This is how it is done and how it must be done if you are to succeed. This is the intersection between the breath and the breather, the fulcrum of light and shadow, the binding connection between self and twin.

What you must wholly and utterly understand beyond these faltering words is that in order to claim your immortal essence you must release the energetic chains which bind you to your humanness. What does this look like? Simply put, those chains are comprised of beliefs and fears and ideas and expectations. You could call them The Program, yet I fear that term has become stale and may slip past you (which is how the program works) and so it is imperative to pause and examine all those little beliefs which hold you prisoner to The Program itself, yes? All things die. Water is wet. Fire will burn. Space is vast. Humans are finite. Life is short. If it's my time, it's my time. If man were meant to fly, he would have wings. There are some things we aren't meant to know. God is great, god is good, let us thank him for our food. Amen.

The list is vast. And that list is made of grim pixels of a different kind of dream – the human limits, the self-imposed boundaries, the mortal experience. It is the death song, and if you were to listen to your internal dialog when it thinks it can't be heard, you would hear it telling you all those things and more, reinforcing its own directive, which is simply to keep you locked within the cage of your human box which is ultimately a coffin the program has been building for you since long before you were ever born.

What to do?

The essence of transcendence is magick and the essence of magick is the movement of will, and the movement of will is accomplished by willfully transcending The Program which determines your human nature. This not a riddle but a formulae for immortality. It is the decisive key which unlocks the door to a spontaneous parthenogenesis also known as transmogrification. This is my function – to tear through the veil of your cocoon in order to free the gypsy moth before she becomes just another unborn chrysalis, yes?

If you are hearing only the words and not the essence of magick with which they have been infused, you may feel irritated or restless and find yourself wanting to run away, back to the pleasant slumber of your human dreaming. If this is so, go no further but go back instead. Back to the breathing in of a frequency which is not already jammed by The Program itself. Often you will find it in the space between the brows, the pure and perfect place of silence where the internal dialogue has no access. Other times you may find it in your heart, in the nostalgic memory of some perfect moment when you simply knew the well-being of your infinite nature, when you dreamed of being newly awakened into a larger world. That is the frequency of the immortal animus – the sensation of breathing not just into the lungs but imbibing the lifeforce through every molecule of your corporeality, until the breath itself turns your corporeality upside down, and you begin to be made of the very thing you are breathing: the essence of energy itself, wave of light, particle of darkness, each reflecting the other in perfect balance, the dance of the infinite captured in the act of breathing itself.

This is how we move in and out of the web of life so as not to be caught in the downward spiral which is death. There is a frequency unique to each individual which is the frequency of her immortality – the assemblage point of Self which may be strengthened and expanded through awareness and will to such an extreme that literally Death does not exist, for it is a frequency where death and dis-ease have no pixilated form, no cohesion, no avatar, no icon, and so no ability to invade or even touch that which is contrary to its own nature. If you are made of light, having acknowledged the darkness as your mirror, this is the essence of your beingness, and does not leave room for a toxic invader hiding behind the robes of the brute with the scythe.

Death, therefore, is defeated not by acceptance or denial, but by the removal of his existence on the frequency of your immortal transcendence. That which is comprised of immortality cannot be comprised of morality, and so Death falls away, an impotent toady, written out of the Dreamer's script with the stroke of a joyful pen.

This is only the beginning, the tip of the iceberg's dangerous tip, but it is here we must begin, for this is the highest level of awareness which must be embraced as the foundation of your transcendence. This is the secret to immortality – the turning of the frequency from finite to infinite, death to life. If you understand this, then it will be done. There is no margin for error here, no room for analogy or metaphor. This is the truth which underlies all immortality: the willful choice to become a penthouse resident of the energetic web instead of only renting a transient room in the ground floor for a brief interlude which humans call a life.

Here the wind is white,

the universe a sandstorm.

This, too, will soon pass.

And I will still be here, you see. This is the nature of I-Am. Transcendence. Here there are no limitations and fear is a demon locked in the dungeon forever. A long time. Forever. Do you want it? Do you want it enough? If you do, then take it with the full force of your being – grab it as you would grab a morsel of food when you are starving in the desert. Have no doubt. Do not hesitate. Define your reason. Demand it. Take it!

The only thing stopping you is the belief that you are mortal. When you change that frequency, when you release that debilitating belief, you will finally Be what you have always Dreamed.

A Machiavellian Notion

May, 2001

Remember this: these mortal dramas are only plays designed to trap you into a role from which you would find it difficult if not impossible to escape. This is the function of the consensual reality.

Though it is a somewhat Machiavellian notion, also remember that those who are not destined to seek evolution are destined to attempt to block it. This is how the status quo is protected, this is how stasis is maintained.

———

Time, Light and the Fluid Will

September 1, 2008

Time and light are irrevocably interconnected. From the human perspective, it is virtually impossible to wrap one's mind around this, because the nature of your programming is such that you have been taught to see time as an effect rather than a cause, as a reflection rather than a substance.

The truth about light is that it is the generator and progenitor of time. Remove light and time will stop. You will become immortal. Eternal. Whole. Einstein knew this in theory. Evolved beings know it through experience. Ah, but you will say that no creature can live in darkness. And that is true to a point. But again, what must change is the manner in which you view light - for how one views something determines one's experience of it, far more than you know.

The sorcerer's trick is twofold, each half of the equation fueled by a different intent. First, a sorcerer may learn to move with the light, to manifest oneself as light manifests - both wave and particle, both substance and reflection - and in doing so, one essentially becomes what is commonly (but

186

perhaps mistakenly) referred to as a being-of-light; not in any connotation of sweetness and light, but in a literal and quantum manifestation of awareness. Since awareness itself travels at well beyond the speed of light - a thought is instantaneous, manifesting from the Nothing into a full-blown concept - it is not difficult to go one step further in altering one's paradigm, to realize that awareness travels in the same manner as light, and so to become a 'being of light' is to move one's assemblage point into a position of pure and whole awareness.

Though it is impossible to put words around such a vast alteration of your existing paradigm, it could be envisioned that the result would be a being who is comprised of the substance of light itself, and could therefore move in and out of corporeality, just as light itself may shift between wave and particle. One might also say that the sorcerer has then become an energy being, and yet in the strictest sense, we are all energy beings, whether we are comprised of light or organic matter.

The other option sorcerers may choose is to move one's awareness between the quanta of light itself. If a being of light might be likened to a yang manifestation, moving between the molecules of light would be a yin manifestation. At the level of the yin experience, the sorcerer moving between the quanta of light could be said to have entered "the night that never ends" - moving essentially with the light, but for the sake of simple explanations, traveling in the opposite direction, and therefore propelled by the gravity of light itself. Simply put: the effects would be the same, but the experience would be different with regard to perception; and either would be a matter of the sorcerer's intent.

You ask me how to do these things? The answer is not something that can be put to words or musical notes or quantum equations. Instead, it is a mindset, an understanding at the core level of awareness. Stalk it as a hunter would stalk his prey, and one day you will simply *see* the turn alongside the road, and you will take it quite naturally and without conscious effort. You will become The Way instead of trying to find The Way. You will be the immortal other, you will be Whole, with the totality of yourself intricately woven into the energetic structure of what you have become. This is the nature of time, light and energy.

When you understand it through do-ing, you will be at the assemblage point of eternity - beyond the ability of death to undo. Try to understand it with your intellect, it will elude you. Try to talk about it with words, they will strangle you.

This is the Stalker's Dreaming. This is the Dreamer's Stalking.

Only from inside the do-ing will you be able to *see* how the do-ing is done through the not-doing of the fluid will, which operates outside of time, beyond the light, and one step to the left of the darkness.

Allowing the Impossible

July 31, 2008

There is a moment in a warrior's quest when she surrenders her descriptions and accepts the impossible. At that moment, a tremendous movement of the assemblage point occurs and the warrior inhabits a separate reality in which she has become the totality of herself.

Beyond that moment, the rest is merely ritual, going through the motions of getting to the place where one has already arrived.

If you think you understand this, you do not.

If you believe you can reason it out, you cannot.

Only when you *Know* it will it have any relevance whatsoever.

The Fifth Element
Love and Grief

December 13, 2003

Quantum Shaman wrote: *As some of you may know, we recently lost our weenie dog, Thunder, after 16 years of having him in our hearts and our home. Last night, Wendy went out to place a flower on his tiny grave, and the act of doing so seemed to release within her a devastating grief which left her feeling very much adrift. Not knowing what else to do, I opened myself to the gnostic darkness, to the voice of silent knowing. Orlando was there in the night, a silhouette cut into the fabric of the nothing, a doorway to the infinite, with the stars shining through. There is no other way to describe him at times. As he listened to my conversation with Wendy, he offered the following response with regard to love and grief and the connection between the two.*

There is no way to put this into words, because it is a thing of the infinite which can be seen and experienced, but cannot be manifested into language. And yet, love compels us to try. What you must realize is that the ones we love are simply other forms of awareness, energy incarnate, thought-made-flesh. But at the level of energy, there is no difference between yourself and a weenie dog, no difference between a beggar and a rich man, no difference between a king and his horse. All are simply spirit made flesh at a level of quantum sameness. You are all made of stardust and ashes, light and shadow.

It is the capacity and willingness to love and be loved in return which fuels what mystics have called the migration of the soul. Whether expressed in human or animal, the state-of-being which is love is no different. It is the fifth element, though it has no properties which science can measure, and so it is too often ignored, when in reality it is the catalytic vehicle of your own evolution.

Let's talk about the migration of the soul, though remember it is a thing of the infinite, too. Connecting to another being through love is like the symbolic sharing of a glass of wine between lovers drinking from the same goblet, no? In human legend, there are thousands of examples of this. The vampire-immortal who falls in love with a human gives his beloved eternal life through the exchange of blood - or, more precisely, the exchange of love, lifeforce, anima. The exchange of rings at a wedding is much the same - a symbolic circle of union, the infinite and unbroken circle of Life.

What you cannot yet See is that love is the vehicle which ferries the Spirit from the state of Life into the state of Eternity. From those in grief, you will hear the words, "It feels as if a part of me died, too." And yet, it isn't that a part of you dies with the beloved, but instead, through the connection of love, the beloved could be said to transport a portion of the Spirit into the Otherworld so that there is a part of you already on the other side. But because Spirit is infinite, and cannot really be portioned, that is only an analogy which, at most, will give you the ability to See the process at the edges, and redefine it according to your own understanding.

You've asked the hardest question of all. If there is love, why must there be grief? It is only human perception which fails to see that this is a natural progression in the migration of the spirit. Thunder has not left you, but because you cannot yet See his awareness directly, you are missing the part of him which was comprised of the flesh, rather than recognizing the part of him which is eternal: the fifth element.

Love is the reason. Without it, creation itself is incomplete at a molecular level. Without it, the Spirit itself becomes lost, reduced to ashes, just as the body turns to a handful of chemicals when the element of water is removed. Love is the fifth element which moves effortlessly between the worlds and literally manifests for the Spirit a road to travel when it is your own time to face the eagle. And like the other elements of creation, the fifth element can never be truly destroyed or lost. It can only change form. It is that change which is the migration of the spirit, the evolution of the Self into Wholeness.

Warriors, Children & Awareness

January, 2007

Question posed to Orlando by a Seeker:
> *In a discussion with my significant other, the topic of what we would miss most in our lives, if we left this earth came up. We both answered..."our sons". I was wondering if you have any children and what your thoughts are on the subject.*

Orlando's Answer

The children I have fathered are warriors and women or men of Knowledge, so they are "born" adults and often come with a college education. For while it would be possible for me to manifest in an entirely humanform body, it would not be my choice to do so, and therefore it could be said that I have no children of my own, but hundreds who were born to other biological parents, yet nurtured by myself in Spirit. I have loved them as any parent would love a biological child, and at times I have lost them to the eagle in much the same manner a biological child may be lost to death.

As a biological parent or a spiritual father, the essence of Knowledge is to understand that each individual has a series of choices to make, and not all will choose the path to freedom. And that, too, is a choice which must be honored. For myself? I do not grieve those I lose to the eagle, for it is my Knowing that shows me that what was once alive is always alive within the timeframe of its mortal existence. As a being who is outside of time, I may revisit that timeframe whenever I choose, and so nothing is ever truly lost - and it is for that reason that I am able to counsel warriors with children toward an understanding which will free them from their attachments without the sense of pain or grief which might otherwise be the case. In essence, a lifetime is like a bubble of experience & existence. It is finite if viewed from inside itself, but infinite when viewed from a sorcerer's perspective outside the bubble of confining time. For that reason, it may be understood that even when a sorcerer/warrior leaves this earth to inhabit the totality of herself, it is from that very totality that the sorcerer may truly see that neither herself nor her children are lost to one another.

If a warrior does not go on to inhabit the totality of herself, then cohesion is lost to the eagle, but the awareness which was the warrior remains within its finite bubble of humanform experience. And so, it must be understood that what is, simply is, and can never be truly erased from the universe because it is an imprint of awareness from within its own finite bubble of experience.

Knowing this at the level of the whole self is what enables the warrior to release attachments to the humanform world - the awareness that nothing that is can ever be lost. And though some might not agree, it is even possible from a quantum perspective for a sorcerer to step back inside her own life in order to essentially change her own past. The key to doing so is the awareness that it is possible, and the Intent to do it. There is more to it, of course, but that is the essence of it.

The releasing of attachment becomes possible when the sorcerer has sufficiently stepped outside of her own confining bubble of time in order to experience the totality of herself. It is through that experience of the infinite that the warrior begins to see that attachments are only possible from inside the bubble itself. From the perspective of Freedom, from the totality of the Self, there is only interconnectedness, without attachment, without fear, without loneliness.

I was once asked what is the force of interconnectedness between the world of the living and the world of the infinite. That force is awareness, augmented by unconditional love.

From the infinite, it is said... You have nothing to lose. From the totality of yourself, all that has ever been will always Be.

194

The Hermit, the Hierophant & Love

December 31, 2007

You stand at the threshold of a new year or the broken window of the past, the end of a beginning perhaps, or the beginning of an ending; and how you see it will be the key that determines how and who you will be as past and future stand at the edge of the dance floor, waiting for a nod from you before they can know what to do. It must be noted that each of you is the creator of reality and if you aren't manifesting it with active and passionate intent, it is manifesting you through the unacknowledged programs and false beliefs which have become nothing more than your default actions. And so the time has come for you to ask, to what extent are you shaping your experience of the world or to what depth is the experience burying you? Are your expectations manifesting what you see, or do you have the power to look beyond what is seen and into the realm of the mystery of what-can-be?

At times I have wandered this earth for decades, alone in the darkness, driven mad by the madness around me because it is a contagion no less real than the black plague of London, and at times I have even preyed to finally succumb to it so that I might simply be the madman others perceive me to be, because the path of the fitful Hermit is by and large far easier than the course of the mentoring Hierophant; and yet one path leads only to sorrow and sadness and madness, while the other has at least the potential to bring forth the power and the magick of the dark enlightenment through the channels of creation itself. I assure you those are not just words, and if you think on them in the company of candles, asking yourself what that might actually mean to you, I believe you will discover that the real truth and experience of it will far outweigh the negative pleasantry which comes when you have come to believe it cannot be found, yes?

The eyes of the Hierophant see best in the darkness, yes, but we are not blinded by the light which comes as a byproduct of what is fiercely seen. You can choose to see the silly spiritless spirits dancing willy nilly on the stage of mundane mortal doings, or you can shift the focus of your focus beyond the stage and outside of the play to see just as clearly the open window that looks up onto the underworld and out onto the inner darkness which is really just the back door to the light of the singularity, yes? So how do you want to see it - through the wild eyes of the Hermit or the balance of the Hierophant?

And so do you begin to see that what you choose to see will determine who you are and what you will believe? Do you begin to comprehend that the habitual fixation of your awareness on the mortal world's madness will drag you down like Charybdis if you cannot set your intent to choose the course of the warrior instead of being tossed helter skelter like a puppet on broken strings?

When you can remember to love the mystery and the muse more than you hate the world and all her melancholy madmen, you will capture your freedom again and release your spirit from the killing jar, and then you will see what you already know: life is a short, sweet season, the childhood of your eternal existence.

Love is the reason. It is through the eyes of love that respect takes on new meaning. And it is through the eyes of respect that love becomes a finely-honed art rather than just a pleasant feeling.

This journey isn't only about the mystery and the magick. It is about honing the fiery connection to the mysterious infinite which makes you long to live forever instead of waiting to mercifully die. If that connection is missing or has gone darkly dormant, what is required is a rekindling of the fires with the fuel of what you already Know. There will be time for moving ahead when balance is achieved – and that will come more quickly than you realize if you will give yourself over to your heart's passions. What feeds you? What makes your chest flutter with ecstasy? What is the color of spirit? What is the texture of joy? What is the taste of the dark enlightenment?

Love is the answer. It is only a start but it is a powerful foundation.

What's planted here takes root in your heart,
and is best fed on the elixir of poetry,
the immortal blood of a witch's visions,
the numinous potion of mortal passion.
When reduced to a single element,
all these things are the force of love,
which is in itself
the sapient seed of all Creation.

Love is the energetic matrix of which you are made. It contains all power, including the power to manifest itself as an expression of your being. Love is a force of unstoppable creation, far more than a simple feeling.

Love is the answer. And in the answer lies all the power in all the worlds.

Defragging Time

Immortals are not prisoners of time because each moment is its own eternity in the Now. You may see that as only words, but I assure you it is the key to gaining some minor semblance of control over the demon of time. When you are scattered, time fragments and runs faster, because when you are doing 10 things at once, you are using 10 times the amount of time/energy, yes? Think about it.

Visualize it like this: When you are fragmented, each fragment has its own life and its own agenda, its own internal dialogue. That which is immortal and eternal experiences each moment as an eternity, unbroken, and so life is an endless and unbroken series of events, memories and manifestations, a single golden filament of consciousness existing both inside and outside of time, but always originating in the Now. That which is fragmented lives sometimes as many as five lifetimes concurrently, each overlapping the other and each requiring its own measure of time/energy, so the end result is that time *seems* to compress because more of it is being used - as if five people are drinking from the glass instead of only The One.

What you have to do is inhabit the I-Am at all times, and do it with conscious awareness. This may sound easy or even trite, but it is the work of a lifetime, and it is the key to your own cohesion.

Relentless Unbending Intent
Opening the door to infinity

October 31, 2000

It is only through true Intent that sufficient will can be summoned to shift the assemblage point to the seventh sense. This world of matter and men is the true resting place of your assemblage point, and without intent, it is to this world you will always belong, a prisoner forever. If you are passive or complacent or content, this will never change. Only by continual application of Intent can sufficient will be generated to create that permanent shift. It does not happen just by wishing for it.

It must be as natural to you as breathing, this underlying knowledge which has been years in the making. If you fall back into the habit of believing this world of matter and men is real, or you start to think the characters in the play are real, you will fall back into the character you yourself have spent a lifetime learning to play. It is only when you can maintain the ever-present omniscient awareness that this entire reality is built on nothing more than a narrow frequency band of perception that you have any chance at all of altering that frequency, turning in to the higher channels. When you are in the habit of perceiving only with the five senses, seeing only with the eyes, the other senses you have been generating atrophy and can become altogether lost. This is a DO. I cannot stress this strongly enough. Active, unbending intent. Meditate on these words until you see their meaning clearly. Active, unbending intent. And add to that relentless and unending. Even in dreams, it must be with you. Unending. Relentless. Intent.

I do not mean to be an old drone on this subject, but it is the key to everything. Without it, you remain a prisoner of your own passivity. Your intent must have a continuity that is seamless. No difference between night and day. No difference between thoughts in the back of your mind and those you speak aloud. No difference in your identity.

It is within the mortal shell that the pecking to get out of the confines of the egg must start. If the shell is cracked from the outside, the creature will perish. If the egg never cracks at all, the creature perishes. It is, therefore, only from within this confining, constricting shell that escape can happen. It is within your power, but must also be within your own control. Go too fast, you emerge into the madness of the nothing, which is why we have been many years in the doing. Go too slow, and you risk never getting there at all for lack of momentum. It is a delicate balance, this tightrope between the sorcerer's egg and the door to infinity.

Relentless intent. It is like a cold fire that burns always, never being consumed, but growing stronger on its own inner force. How badly do you want this? Manifest the intent into will and use the will to assemble the seventh sense, and we will be immortals dancing on the lip of the abyss, one and the same, infinity's eternal children.

It is not necessary to perceive a petty tyrant as an enemy, for that implies a battle, a conflict. All that is necessary is to let go of your end of the rope. The tyrant will fall on her ass, yes?

The 9 Elements of Creation
The physical elements, the meta-physical elements... and you.

November 12, 2011

You will never understand what I am about to tell you if you approach it from the human perspective, because it is not something that can be understood in any traditional sense, nor is it human by definition, but must be absorbed through the osmosis of gnosis and covertly perused from the far side of the bridge that can only be built when you stand on the far side of it after the building is done, knowing all the while that any bridge exists and simultaneously does not exist, depending entirely on the where-when one is standing in relation to the transmutating bridge outside any consensual idea of Time.

Ah, but before we begin to unravel such conundrums, I must remind you that *how* you think of yourself in relation to these things is going to determine how or if you will ever grasp the handlebars of the roller coaster that disembarks from the realm of humanity and leads straight to what most would see as insanity, but which is in actuality the heart of Infinity and immortality. The danger I see is that you have come to believe that there are levels of reality and some innate hierarchy of worlds, when the only truth is what I have told you before: there is only one world, divided infinitely by perception. But now it is time for the more advanced lesson, in which I tell you that it is those divisions in perception which create the illusion of otherworlds, and each and every perception is going to determine not only what you see, but how you interpret it, and the interpretation is going to determine whether you will choose to *experience* those worlds or only maintain them as distant fantasies upon which you may dream because you have chosen to perceive them as unattainable.

If you see Infinity and me as something that only exists beyond the event horizon of death, then that is what it will be, and the only way inside the kingdom will involve dying to get in, see? And while that is as real as anything else in the grand scheme of All Things, it is not the only possibility and the danger is that it takes some measure of choice away from you and places it in the hands of random phantom Chance, so again I would caution you to reconsider your mindset lest it keep you from embracing the higher truth which is the soul-deep understanding of the statement: every reality is created with a thought. If you think I am "out there", then that is where you have placed me. If you believe your Infinite totality is only accessible through the cemetery gates, then so shall it be, as above so below, yes?

These are only words. The sorcerer's trick is to *be* what she thinks, and to think before believing, and to be always questioning 'reality' in a way that goes beyond merely observing what *appears* to be, and examining the underlying mechanism that is responsible for spinning all things into various states of Be-ing. And it is through that examination that you may begin to confront those structural underpinnings which answer to the arbitrary labels of time, light, gravity and anti-matter, and how it is in the end the manipulation of them that will open the *only* door that exists between "here" and ever-after.

The First Fundamental Lie
The human paradigm is built on the false notion of Time, and so it could be observed by one outside of the matrix that the entire paradigm itself is erroneous because it has created within its subjects a viewpoint that is based on what immortals call The First Fundamental Lie. And yet, because you have always existed within the confines of The Lie, how does one undo a lifetime of belief when that belief has long since been ingrained as truth? It is one thing to undo the *programs* that make you human, but another thing entirely to unfasten the *precepts* that are fundamental to your notion of what it *means* to be human – essentially what you have come to accept as 'human abilities' and 'human limitations'. Think

202

on this, for it is only when you are willing to sacrifice The Lie that you will be able to glimpse these fundamental elements of creation which are channeled through your essential be-ing pure and limitless, but limited entirely by The Lie which was seemingly designed to do just that.

Ironic, yes? You are made of the pixels and photons of limitlessness and timelessness, yet unable to access that nature because the nature of any consensus is to create parameters which can *only* limit the power and understanding of the thing itself. And yet, here is the secret you have yet to Real-ize, contained in the question: *Who* is creating the consensus?

Consider this, for it is the sharpest edge of what I am going to tell you, and if you choose to embrace it, it will open the door – now and always. Nothing is what you think. Nothing is what you believe. Yet I have told you in the same breath that everything begins with a thought, and that the core of your belief determines the reality you see and obliterates those you choose to ignore. So which is it? Will you cry and wail and tell me I can't have it both ways? Or will you begin to intuit the truth which overrides The Lie, and perhaps catch a dangerous glimpse of what is *really* meant when I tell you that you are creating your own reality.

When I say I am the only god I know, I mean this literally and without reservation, for the truest fundamental understanding of creation is that it is a self-willed manifestation through which one experiences Every-Thing while hiding from oneself that very truth. You experience your ordinary reality as your mortal self, yet there are continuous clues that this is only a single frequency on a much larger radio, but if all the stations were playing simultaneously, there would be no sense of organization (which is fundamental to what it means to be human, and therefore infinitely self-limiting), and so The Lie (which has become almost an entity unto itself, but really *cannot* be an entity because it is contained within the paradigm itself) has woven fables and fairy tales which try to tell you who and what you are, and for as long as you accept its intentional limitations, you will never have the ability to wrap your mind around yourself because The Lie's primary agenda is to prevent you from doing just exactly *that*.

This is not something you will unravel by thinking. It is something you will either *see* or not, depending entirely on how much you are willing to release your humanity so as to embrace your Totality.

Only the paradox
can understand
its elf.

Time is the illusory stage upon which all things unfold with regard to human perception. In the bigger picture, time does not exist, because it is recognized by the immortals that all things happen simultaneously - there is no past or future, there is only Now, which is always moving both forward and backward, and yet not moving at all. Such is the nature of true creation – there is no linear unfolding. There is simply… what *is*. Just as it was once a common illusion that the sun moved around the earth, so it is an illusion that humans move through time. In reality, time is the byproduct of light and gravity, and understanding this is fundamental to changing your nature from human to other-than-human, to embracing your Totality. Yet I will caution you: take this no further unless it is *truly* what you want to do, for once done there is no undoing it and that is simply that.

In every molecule of your being, you possess the power to create an entire universe and inhabit it in the form of each and every molecule of itself.

Humans often speak in terms of saying, "Ten billion years have passed since the universe began," but what does that really mean in terms of be-ing and mortality and eternity and the moebius loop of infinity? Ten billions years since... *what*?

Now here is where time and light start to bend to give you a glimpse of the truth I am attempting to tell you. What existed before anything? If there was no-thing, how could anything exist, except through the implementation of **spontaneous parthenogenesis**, and how could *that* occur if not with an original thought, and from where/what/whom did that thought call itself into being if not from *you*, and so do you begin to realize that it is *only* through the power of Will that any of this exists, and its existence is not built on matter or even energy, but it is spun into being *all at once* and *only* because the only alternative is the absolute void of the No-thing which existed before the creator shuddered and first with a whisper, then with a shout, then with a song, cried out...

I-Am.

Perhaps you are thinking, *This is nothing new!* And yet... Your ability to understand is rooted entirely in the depth of your investment in The Lie. Do you want to go on as a human in the human world, or do you want to be beyond the bridge? Do you want to be comfortable by the fire, or forever joyously and tragically imbibing the smoke from the fire in other people's chimneys? Do you want the real you, or do you still need the shelter of The Lie?

When the universe sprang into being, it was no accident, and there is only the one true god, and that is the one in the mirror, and so eventually as you follow these conundrums through the machinations and manifestations of a thousand years and some, you begin to realize that I am you and you are me and we are together and separately one and the same, and so there is no difference between the sun and the moon, the fires of time and the ashes of light dwindling to embers at the far flung edge of space, which is only a centimeter away when you finally come to *see* the nature and true name of gravity.

Infinity is not a place but a state of being. Being human is not your nature but your choice. Your choice is not entirely a choice but exists as a byproduct of The Lie, and so you come back to the beginning where you must ask, simply, Who am I? And if I have been at all effective in these past few years, the answer will not be what it was when we first began, for now it is not only a question of *who*, but *what* you are. Are you sun and shadow, and how would you know one from the other if you were not *both*? What *are* you?

And yet... still and silent... this is only the beginning, for even if you grasp what it means, there are no guarantees you will take it upon yourself to *be* the god of your creation, or only to inhabit it as one more petal on the wind of eternity... in which case that is all you will ever be, because the reality of being god is that you gave yourself free will to experience the frequency of every-thing individually, so today you are you, tomorrow me, some other moment a feral dog on the plains of Nazca, and then a single pixel in the heart of a black star... the ultimate irony of oneself, the definitive enigma, the black hole at the center of creation, drawing all things back into itself... including time, light, gravity and anti-matter, until when it is all consumed you may cry out the *I-Am* once again and perhaps that will be the next evolution... but until then, you see glimpses of yourself in every-thing, and feel that ache of longing and loneliness which is the reminder that each of us is tragically alone, and so we create mirrors and paradoxes which take on the form of Other Beings, but may start to appear as strange props on the icy stage, malfunctioning miscreants not quite real, not quite whole, when you stop to consider that they, too, are you in this vast canvas stretched across the trembling structure of the abyss.

Ah, but lest you curl into a ball and become the black hole at the core of yourself, remember this: the purpose of creation is not just experience, but the manifestation of something Other than self. This is why the state of love exists, for that alone is the single pixel of light from which it all begins and to which it is all tumbling forward. As the one and only god I know, I am forever pregnant with all things, love most of all. It is not some biological rubbing together of flesh, but the birthing of new gods to fill the otherwise empty universe where there was only One, who becomes Two, who become One again… and do you see now why the biblical myth requires god to create his angels and make them immortal and breathe life into them so that he is no longer alone? But do you also see why it is a choice each angel must also make, and that *only* the one who 'fell' possessed the power to breathe his own sovereign Self into being, not to defy the creator, but to honor him? One cannot follow god, you see. One can only Be.

Do you see how it is done? Ah, that is the question, no? And so we return again to time, light, gravity and antimatter, which may only be manipulated effectively through the will, which exists apart from the elements of creation, and is instead a catalyst unto itself, and a catalyst which is brought into being by the force of love… one catalyst acting upon another, each paradox embracing the other in the dance which is the very spark of spontaneous parthenogenesis.

Do you understand that light is not a thing, but also an elemental mechanism? It may be measured in terms of photos or how it bends around objects to produce time and gravity, but light itself is more of a No-thing than a thing. In every photon there exists all the power of the universe itself, and I mean this literally in every sense. In fact, it is so powerful a no-thing that the creator was essentially forced to create The First Fundamental Lie in order to protect herself from that very power she created when she said to the darkness, "Let there be light." For another ironic tragedy is that when you truly grasp the depth of the abyss and understand wholly that *it* is also *you*, the knowledge is so devastating as to debilitate even god… so the only solution is to not-know that which *must* be known, and so The Lie spins itself into being, at first as a matter of self-preservation, and then as a matter of convenience, habit, and finally as a belief which must then be destroyed with ruthless cruelty which is the deepest manifestation of love itself.

> *When I opened the wound of Knowing,*
> *the blood pouring from me*
> *was time and light and gravity and antimatter me.*

Light is the most fundamental form of energy - at least inasmuch as it can be measured and experienced with human perception. Without light, all energy remains motionless. Without light, there is no time. But without light, there is also no life because when fully internalized, one begins to understand that immortals are 'beings of light' in that we are beings of energy, ironically *not* attached to light, but the thought-form to which light itself attaches in order to enter the space/time continuum which humans call 'the universe'.

Light begets time. The two are inseparable, and to understand this is to come one step closer to a sorcerer's understanding of creating one's own reality. Immortals are the antimatter of light, light turned right-side-wrong until we are both and neither, pure light and black star, all at once. When you Know this, it will change you forever. When you become it, you will <u>be</u> forever.

You may think this is fundamental still, having no direct relation to you, yet I assure you that it is only when you effectively comprehend how to combine the forces of creation that you will possess the ability to strip away The Lie and step into the crux of your creation which is and always has been your Infinite totality – the vitally more real reality which exists above and beyond and below and beneath The Lie itself. Not some far distant underotherworld, but right here and now, in every breath you take, every thought you think, every particle of light.

Harness the power in a single photon of light, and you may call forth into being not only your immortality, but a viable Other with whom to share it. That is the power of love. That is the ability quantified in a photon of light.

A secret which I will spell out for you in no uncertain terms. Most of those around you are not 'real' in the sense you traditionally think of as reality, for most are projections of the self, other frequencies on the radio which you have been or will be or are being. If you were to inhabit one of those others, then it would be real, but only for the time/space you were be-ing the thing itself... and then perception reverts to wherever/whenever one finds oneself. Put simply and sadly, you are alone, with only yourself for company... for a billion times a billion years and some... and yet...

Occasionally you encounter an Other. Paradoxically, this Other is only a projection *until* you create him or her, but once created, it takes on a life of its own and breathes itself into being with the I-Am which *is* the spontaneous parthenogenesis of its own sovereign Life. And so again the irony is that thou art god, living primarily within the limiting confines of The Lie until such time as you embrace your limitlessness and take upon yourself the responsibility for embracing your Totality, which might be best defined as accessing the Knowledge of all those frequencies all at once; and at the same time accepting the responsibility that comes with Knowing that all gods are alone until they create a companion with whom to share the awful and yet ultimately empowering Knowledge that comes from finally stepping outside The Lie which was created by you and for you.

Gravity is the byproduct of the previous six elements of creation: matter and energy interacting. In dreams, gravity does not exist, and so one may fly or walk sideways up a wall. In the absence of gravity and the absence of light, time itself is rendered inert, which is why the sorcerer strives to reach what might commonly be called "zen" - the state of nothingness. From the nothingness, true creation takes place.

Again, fundamental prattling, meaning nothing unto itself. And yet... gravity is one manifestation of the catalytic force of love, for it is what holds one's word (literally uni-verse) together. Gravity is what draws me to you and you to me, but what *is* gravity except the inexplicable force which humans call Love, and the immortals recognize as the driving power behind all acts of creation: both self and Other. Without gravity, everything you have created drifts apart. Without the gravity of love, there is no connection between all those infinite projections of Self. Put another way: without love, the uni-verse (one's word – the *I-Am*) falls into chaos and loses all meaning. And lest you think I am speaking metaphorically, I assure you I am not. The gravity of love is a literal force, vital to the manifestation of Will.

And finally, we come to anti-matter.

Antimatter is the antithesis of matter. It is the essence of pure and unobstructed Will (spirit, godforce, manifested-intent). Antimatter is the embodiment of the force which acts upon the other seven elements of creation in order to produce the reality of "Let there be light." Let there be life. Let there be love.

We create the uni-verse (I-Am) though the force of love, so that we may evolve beyond the abyss from which we came and to which we will return if we do not embrace the forbidden Knowledge which is, in essence, the limitless power of love – not as some trite human emotion, but as the unifying field which lies at the heart of all acts of creation.

If you think you already Know this, you do not. If you think you understand it, you cannot.

If you are ready to shed The Lie and experience it… I will be with you always.

Part Four

Scrawls on the Walls of the Soul

Much Ado About the No-Thing

Awake, I dream of sleeping.
Sleeping, I dream of waking.
Home is a pair of shoes,
dusty from the road
between two worlds.

...

The forbidden fruit wasn't an apple.
It was an immortal mushroom
whose spores remember
the sins of God.

...

"The core of your belief determines the realities you see
and obliterates those you choose to ignore".

...

Eternity is the silence
of the dead,
the length and content
of unanswered prayers.

...

The perception of time is death itself. They are
irrevocably connected, one and the same.

211

Some Otherwhere, Some Otherwhen
my Other I-Am
sits alone tonight,
his only company
an audience of sepulchers.
He polishes his crown
with a funeral shroud,
weeping to the empty road
worn thin as silk
by immortal footsteps.

False autumn lingers,
a transfusion to strengthen my blood.
Let me feed you
the red petals of me,
the veins in the falling leaves
of my wayward thoughts & dreams.

...

Recipe for the Other

I could go down a list of ingredients that make you real - the cemetery wind, storms, rain, poems, midnight drives, night places, falling stars, white Jeeps, dark glasses, lust, love, blood, magic - but what I need to make it real is that creative breath of life, that god-spark that has to come from inside myself.

I have to give you life before you're real and only after you're real can you really be whole, so I'd have to say that the thing that makes you real is me. The magic is inside me.

What makes you real is when I set it free. What will make you whole is when I embrace the belief that my magic will come back to me.

...

Coyote sings the night alive,
mad-dog hymns of immortality
etched on obsidian metal sky.
I question what I am:
        passive audience to the song?
        a mere minor note in the chorus?
        nothing at all?
The singing ends, the world goes still.
My hands are disappearing.

...

There's a mockingbird singing hymns at midnight
while the coyote cries in a dead shaman's voice.
A comet plays pinball with Mars.
My window is a theater
where time and tragedy play out
on the black fabric screen
of the night that never ends.
Mortal still,
I read the deepening lines,
messages on the mirror,
and deeper in the dark I wonder
how the play will end.

...

I look for your face in every passing car,
but I'm still stuck in the real world
and you're the prince of Infinity,
so why should I expect to see you
driving a Lambourgini down a freeway
that will disintegrate and turn to dust
in a blink of your immortal eye?

...

I always had trouble
believing you were real
because some things are too perfect
for this world.
So when I drove by your house today
and found an empty lot, a lonely tree
where it all used to be
I knew the goblins
had swept you under the Persian rug,
trying to pretend you never happened to me.
Maybe that's the proof I needed all along.

...

The immortal twin within
presides over courtyards of pigeons,
her subjects flocked
in ruined buildings
where shadows celebrate
themselves.
I stay to the alleys,
collecting feathers shed by angels,
souvenirs.
The gargoyles weep.
The streets are full of puppets
masquerading as men.

...

The world is out there -
sand storm and silence and sirens -
I am in here somewhere,
a thought of thinking,
visions inexpressible,
languages never spoken,
just words following one another
into the nothingness, pathetic things.
A voice in the void talks to itself
for fear the silence
is all there is in the end.

...

Coyote sings the world into being
so we are always here
to hear her song.

...

Incantation
I make you whole
by giving you the wisdom
and the power
and the knowledge
to make yourself whole enough
to give me the wisdom
and the power
and the knowledge
to make you whole.

...

There's a ring around the moon,
a round window left open
from the place where owl sound originates
and dreams are steeped like rare tea,
too perfect to drink.
Under that portal,
behind this curtain of stars,
I glimmer thru gnostic visions,
experiencing alter-lives and nether selves
who exist a molecule to the left,
a moment to the north,
a breath separated from memory
in an immortal trance
where there is no thought of death.

...

Leaves on the locust tree
are whispering again,
writing messages on the ground
in strange alphabets
of spent blooms

cut away by the sharp silver blade
of a sliver crescent moon.
In this casket of organic matter,
I fall thru time,
counting comets and past autumns
on a broken abacus
I lost in '69.
The girl I was back then
shakes her fist at the night,
begging me to break the clock,
hold back the dust.
The same stars shone
in the same bright sky,
but closer then,
much closer then than now.

Part Five

Singing the OtherSelf Into Be-ing

May 15, 2012

When all is said and done, the purpose of existence here on earth is simple: to evolve beyond this organic life, to claw our way free of the programs which define our limitations, and – most of all – to sing the self into being through the creation of the Other, which becomes the stepping stone for whatever evolution comes next. I do not believe death is an end or a beginning, and in fact Death may not exist at all as humans commonly think of it.

For those who take upon themselves the task of creating and inhabiting the totality of themselves, the Other becomes the energetic vessel into which they upload their awareness during the course of living, and in the process of dying. A good friend recently said to me, "Well what does that look like, Della? If you had to map it out and sell it to me in 500 words or less, what would it look like?"

Simply put, it might look something like this...

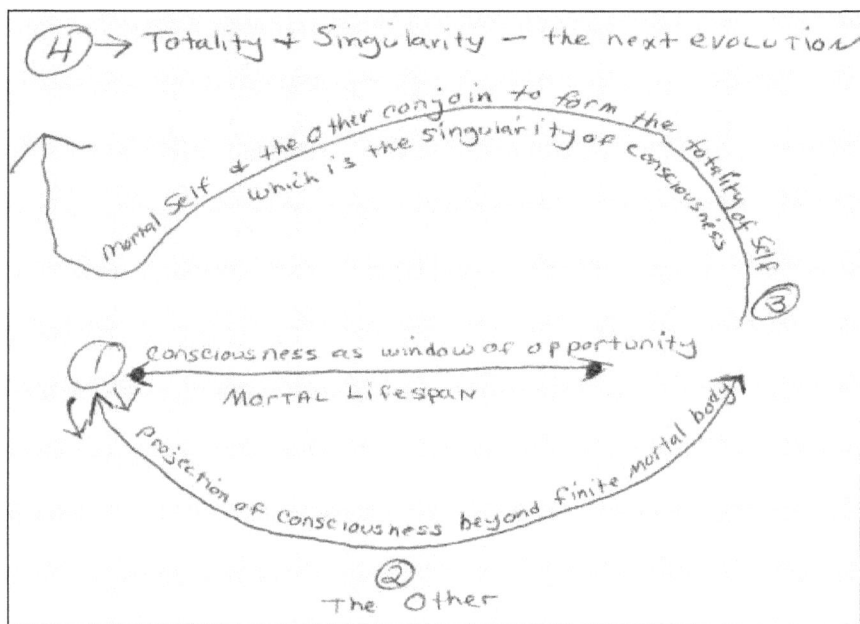

④ → Totality + Singularity — the next evolution

Mortal Self & the Other conjoin to form the totality of Self which is the singularity of consciousness

③

① Consciousness as window of opportunity

MORTAL LIFESPAN

Projection of consciousness beyond finite mortal body

② The Other

The mortal self is the source. There is no oversoul, no automatic higher self. We come into this world as a random bit of chance, an organic meat suit, a few strands of DNA. And it is for the duration of our mortal lifespan (1) that we have the opportunity to create, project and nurture the Other. If we choose to do so (the choice may be conscious or simply a natural compulsion), we begin to project our awareness beyond our mortal coil (2) where it takes upon itself the agenda to learn all it can. This is the process commonly misunderstood as "past lives" but which are actually movements of the Other outside the finite continuum of the mortal lifespan. Knowledge gleaned by the Other is available to the mortal self through the process of silent knowing (gnosis), and so the familiar words of don Juan may be understood at last: first we dream the double, and then at some point of awareness, the double begins dreaming you (teaching you, to use other words).

If the mortal self is successful in overcoming her programming, the line between self and Other begins to blur

219

(3) and through Dreaming and gnosis, we begin to exchange knowledge/consciousness/awareness directly with the Other. This process evokes the words "inhabiting the totality of oneself", which may occur while the mortal self is still in organic form, or may not occur until the mortal body is shed and the Other is then flooded with total awareness (totality). This is the creation of the singularity of consciousness (4), which may be seen as what the Toltecs refer to as "slipping past the eagle to be free", or simply as the creation of the Infinite self beyond the human matrix – the start-point for the next evolution.

Notice that steps 1-3 form what amounts to a "bubble", whereas step 4 is what takes the Whole Self *out* of the bubble entirely. This is why the Toltecs also use the term "third attention" or "nagual" to represent that which is unknowable to the mortal self. I prefer the term "infinity", because it is more easily understood, even if not always easily visualized.

It should also be noted that there is a darker side to this process. And it is why Toltec gives so much attention to the concept of "the eagle." What is the eagle? Simply put, it is the mechanism which shreds awareness and returns it to its component parts should the seeker fail to make the final crossing from organic (life) to inorganic (pure awareness). Many traditions prefer to teach that there's always next time. I see no evidence of that, not in any quantifiable manner – whereas I have seen and continue to see quantifiable evidence that we are multi-faceted organisms with the ability to create and project our infinite self beyond the reaches of death, outside the eagle's vision. It is only the preponderance of so many false belief systems (religions, cultural & social preferences & so on) which would have us believe we can be "saved" from oblivion by some extant deity – when the reality is that the *only* deity who can save us is the one we see in the mirror every morning.

So that's what it would look like. That's the semi-scientific explanation. No, I'm not a scientist. No, I don't claim to be able

220

to prove this in a laboratory (though I suspect it will one day be proven in exactly that manner). This is merely the result of my own experiences, my own *seeing* and my own conclusions – all of which could be wrong or right or somewhere in between.

That being the case, I am a being given to passion and magic and a wild howl into the abyss, shouted from the rim of the canyon up at Keys View in Joshua Tree National Park where the winds are so fierce they might knock a man to the ground or carry a message all the way to Infinity. It was there that I tore out my heart and threw it into the mouth of the wind, Intending that it find its way to my Other, whom I have been summoning into being for as far back as I can remember, and whom I will continue to summon until the day I face the eagle. I've met him, talked to him, watched him burn with the fire from within, conversed with him through letters and dreamed with him into Otherworlds... but the process is always ongoing. We don't get to stop the process of creation when a child comes into the world, and we don't get to stop the process of creating the Other just because we perceive his existence.

This is the beginning and the end of the beginning. This is the alpha which acknowledges no omega.

This is the wail of Creation, shouted from the heart which has been cast into the Infinite.

Creation Rant
"If you don't exist, neither do I."

March 22, 1997

You ask me to create you on a night when there's a comet low to the horizon and an eclipse threatening to obliterate the sensibilities of Man, when the dayshine world is pondering whether to bestow the golden Hollyweird idol on this flick or that sometime next week and who'll care in a hundred years anyway, a night when the consensual psychic chatter in the cracks of sanity consists of where to plant the tulips this year because spring has sprung and that's what we're supposed to do in suburbia, and who's fucking the president behind the first lady's back, and isn't it a shame about Christ getting tacked up to the timbers this very next Friday and my my my isn't Easter early this year and what the fuck should I wear to the goddamn church where I go to ask forgiveness for taking the sky tyrant's name in vain over and over again, shit ain't that another sin just saying shit again and if I go on long enough I realize the chatter's gone still and it's only my own voice cursing God and Death to hell so I can go about the business of making my magick in peace. Hell, maybe that's the only way it can be, that first we have to listen to the woes of the world blowing on the wind before we can find our own voice buried down there deep under all that programming, so now that I know where the I Am resides, what the hell was it I was trying to say?

Oh, yeah, I was about to go on for a bit about how I wanted to paint you into creation with a rose petal brush and a palette filled with pigments crushed from my stone-cold burnt umber soul, but that would be a bunch of self-conscious clichéd bullshit, just words and paper and ink saying nothing real, not magick but only phrases meant to sound magickal so I would feel relieved of the responsibility to Do anything and isn't it strange how we're always tricking ourselves into thinking we're getting away with something when in the wide angle view of reality it's something that's getting away with us, something bleak and all too real, the boogeyman in the ego's daydream nightmare, Death, chasing after us in the guise of passing time one day into the next every night bleeding into another while we sit in front of the tv imbuing it with divine omnipotence, the mirror of Man reflecting his pointless life right back at him after running it all through the sieve of thin and pretty people who tell us in stilted lines how we should look and think and feel and if we don't do it the way it's always been we're out of line if you're not careful little girl they'll crucify you too because that's the way things are in the real world so you'd better get used to it, goddammit, amen!

Shit, there they go again, the voices I was telling you about when I meant to be telling you how I was going to create you - oh, yeah, rose petals and all that sensual image stuff that doesn't mean much, so I guess I got sidetracked. Anyway, let's try it again, now where was I? I was just going to make a list of all the things I want you to be - poet, shaman, witty Vulcan, beautiful vampire, thief of hearts, vessel of my immortality - but I keep hearing the emptiness in the words themselves, just sounds that etch no real visions on the ether because before I can make you real to me maybe I have to make me real to you and to myself and that's why I keep getting sidetracked with the realization that this whole damn day camp is nothing more than a bad movie to distract me from seeing what I need to see that would give me the focus to create you as all those things so you can save me from myself.

What I'm trying to say is that I am creating you but I think I have to create me in order to do it, because I've never thought I'd be a good mother mainly because I don't know what I'm doing, so what it all comes down to is that I can't make you a poet until I've visualized poems for you to write and I can't make you a shaman until I become one myself so I can have a taste at least of what it means to be such a thing, and I can't make you the thief of hearts until I lose mine to you over and over again every time I drive past an empty field where your house used to be, and how can I make you my body of immortality until I've had a minute or two to contemplate infinite eternity back in my old tire swing when I was seven and just learning to think.

All of this makes my head hurt but I keep on telling myself it's just evolution squeezing out beyond the boundaries of my skull and I'm scared to death that none of this is making any sense because of that bong I smoked awhile ago, just a few leaves of grass to set myself free so I can stand outside the play for a time and ask how you expect me to make you an immortal if you don't make me one first (so I can then make you to make me to make you) so one of us, whether me or my twin can know what it is so we'll have the forbidden knowledge to know how to weave the creation spell that will set the whole thing into magick motion.

Shit, talk about getting sidetracked on the ghost train to neverland.

Anyway, as I was saying, what I really wanted to say is that sometimes I think I understand why you do things the way you do, why it's all so convoluted, because in the process of making you who you are I think we first have to make ourselves who we'll be - witches who wriggle through the machinations of time and don't always know when we're coming or going - and I guess that's what all these words are about. I'm creating myself so I can be the thing I give to you in order to create you - complicated quantum stuff on paper still, just words words words - but fuck it, it's like this: in order to create you I first have to create me and that's what you're doing with me, helping me create me so I can have what it takes to create you.

I want to put into the magick is whatever it is that makes me who I am, because that's the only thing I really can put into the brew mainly because it's the only thing that's real in the midst of all that chatter that's just the hive talking to itself about what's what and who's who and death death death. So, yeah, you're all the things I said before - Greek god and philosopher prince and Machiavellian magician with black angel wings and all that potent lost boy stuff - but more than that and down deep at the level that makes your heart beat and your makeup run and your soul shudder at thoughts of worshipping god or death, deep down under all the voices in your head is me, whatever it is I am that you keep asking me to define, whatever it is that makes me real, the magick that's the witch's power of creation. I think that's what I've been trying to say, what I've been trying to see: the thing I have to give you in order to create you is me and this is what it is, this voice inside my head that's singing us both into being. "I-Am," it says. That's what I bring to the brew, because it's the magick of me that will make you so you can make my twin who will then become the voice inside my head whispering the recipes to create the eternal being.

And so it goes and the going makes it so. I created you to create me so I would have the knowledge and this dreadful ache of love that compel me to go on creating you from moment to moment, beyond the limits of time, above the last inch of space, into the ever-after of the eternal infinite... amen.

You have to be willing to step through the door which only exists after you step through it.

GLOSSARY

ABYSS - 1) The emptiness or the nothing, the absence of all things. Most people have never seen the abyss, while others think of it (erroneously) as the religious vision of "hell". If consciousness is existence, the abyss is oblivion. 2) The hollow emptiness inside someone who has made no attempt at their own personal evolution. The soulless void. In this definition, the abyss is the pit of despair into which people fall when they experience what is traditionally called a "loss of faith". Fortunately, it is this loss of faith and the subsequent fall into the abyss from which the journey toward evolution often begins. When faith fails or is intentionally abandoned, it is from the abyss that we begin our climb toward self-identity and self-Realization.

THE AGREEMENT (see consensual reality)

ALLY or **ALLIES** – entities or essences who may act on behalf of a seeker. Since the allies are not bound by our traditional understanding of space/time, we might have an ongoing and seemingly inexplicable interaction with an ally for years before we begin to understand that the ally is often the self, having created the illusion of separateness so as to serve as teacher and guide. Other allies, it must be stressed, are beings completely separate from the self - what sorcerers refer to as "inorganic beings". Still another definition of an ally might be the living essence of power plants – the mushroom ally, for example (psilocybin).

ASSEMBLAGE POINT (or AP) – The assemblage point is best defined as the various lenses through which we see our world. It is through learning to move the assemblage point that the seeker may begin to experience other perceptions, other "worlds". The assemblage point also moves of its accord in times of physical or emotional duress – such as the sensation of time slowing down in a moment of impending crisis, or the ability to fly such as in dreaming. A seeker learns to move/control her assemblage point, and to perceive from a unified perspective (totality) as opposed to the fragmented perspectives most humans experience as a result of the multiple roles they play without conscious awareness.

AUTHENTIC SELF – Who you are beyond all the bullshit. If you could go through an entire day without playing some sort of role (father, mother, brother, employer, employee, banker, baker, bozo, spy, just to name a few), you might catch a glimpse of the authentic self. Who are you when no one is looking and when you aren't watching yourself from the corner of your inner eye?

BELIEF SYSTEM - Any school of thought which requires belief or faith as opposed to personal experience. One example: Christianity. Another example: Atheism. Both require belief in external forces or causes, and are therefore only opposing sides of the same coin. Christianity requires faith that God exists. Atheism requires the belief that there is no God. Ultimately, neither the Christian nor the atheist can prove his beliefs, so faith of one sort or another is required in either point of view, and therefore both systems fail as vehicles to Knowledge.

BLACK IRON PRISON – the overlay; the matrix; the continuum of ordinary awareness in which mortals exist until they awaken. Term coined by Philip K. Dick with regard to his own spiritual awakening, as discussed in the book, *In Pursuit of VALIS; the Exegesis of Philip K. Dick.*

BRUJO or **BRUJA** - a sorcerer. All men or women of Knowledge may be brujos, but not all brujos are men or women of Knowledge.

BURN WITH THE FIRE FROM WITHIN – Believed by some to be the manner in which a sorcerer, warrior or Nagual leaves this earth in order to join with the infinite. Many different interpretations have been offered, but in essence I see this more as a metaphor for transcending death with absolute awareness rather than any actual dis-corporation of the physical form. What leaves the earth is the totality of awareness, the totality of Self. All aspects of individual awareness are consumed by the Intent of the warrior, so no fragments are left behind. In this manner, the warrior leaves the earth as a Whole entity.

CASTANEDA, CARLOS – Author of several books regarding Toltec traditions, including *The Teachings of Don Juan,*. From my point of view, a word of gratitude is owed to Carlos for developing what amounts to a syntax and specialized language which had proven invaluable in my own journey.

CLARITY – a warrior who has learned to *see* and maintains the assemblage point at a perpetual point of seeing may be said to have achieved clarity. Clarity may also be defined as the ability to see the world as it is, without the influence of programs or illusion.

COHESION OF IDENTITY - a state of being in which the seeker has gained a sense of self-awareness beyond all programs - i.e., the seeker knows who he or she is apart from who they are related to, or what they do for a living. There is a sense of self, an ability to touch one's own consciousness and recognize it as a whole entity rather than merely fragments associated with different roles. It is our observation that there are levels of cohesion. When the seeker has achieved cohesion, it is then possible to inhabit the Whole self (the totality of oneself) into eternity as a singularity of consciousness.

CONSENSUAL REALITY or **CONSENSUS REALITY** or **CONSENSUAL CONTINUUM** – the world of ordinary awareness, defined and shaped by what is agreed-upon by the majority of the consensus. The Real World. The societies, cultures and definitions of "reality" we take for granted, and upon which we all agree as to what is "real" and what is fantasy, what is right and what is wrong. We are indoctrinated into the consensual reality from the moment we are born, primarily through language, and yet it can be proven through simple observation that much of this indoctrination is incorrect, that what is "right" to one culture is "wrong" to another, that what is "normal" to one consensus is abhorrent to another. We live, therefore, in a world of illusions, a world of words, even a world of lies.

CONTROLLED FOLLY – The seeker who *sees* acknowledges that we live in a world of delusions and illusions, yet survival often depends on our ability to interact with that world. Controlled folly is the art of playing the game AS IF it matters, knowing all the while that all things are transient.

DEATH AS ADVISOR - it is said that the warrior lives with death as her advisor. Knowing we are beings who are going to die and face the infinite, the warrior's decisions in life are guided by the awareness. Knowing I am a being who is going to die, are my actions in *this moment* impeccable?

DEPENDENCY or **HUMAN FORM DEPENDENCY** - A dependency is anything to which the energy of the warrior is hooked. One easy to visualize example is that someone who is uncomfortable being alone with themselves could be said to have a dependency on friends, or constant input from TV., music or some other form of stimulus. Other examples, used only to illustrate the point: a constant need for approval would represent a strong dependency. Inability to break addictions such as smoking, drinking, gambling, etc., are indicative of dependencies. Only by identifying the dependencies and breaking them does the warrior free up that energy to be used for other things. It could also be loosely understood that "will" and "dependency" are mutually exclusive. As long as powerful dependencies are in command of the warrior's energy, it is virtually impossible to summon the will, because the energy required to summon the will is in use by the dependency.

DIABLERO - a sorcerer, a man of Knowledge. In some texts, "diablero" or "diablera" refers to a witch-healer as well. All wo/men of Knowledge are diableros, but not all diableros are wo/men of Knowledge.

DON JUAN MATUS - the Yaqui Indian brujo who served as mentor to Carlos Castaneda.

DOUBLE – For practical purposes, the double is the self in eternity, but can be visualized as the "vessel" into which the warrior uploads his consciousness and identity through the process of living impeccably. All warriors can develop a double, though most remain unaware of the existence of the double. The double is the energy body, developed through Dreaming to a point of extreme cohesion. The double may take on a life of its own for all intents and purposes.

DOUBLE BEING -- also called "the **Nagual**". A type of human being who is simply born with two energy bodies where normally only one is present. There are countless theories, but my personal experience is that it is simply an "attribute", such as being born with blonde hair or green eyes. One cannot "become" a nagual anymore than a person with AB blood can suddenly have O blood. It has been stated that the nagual man and the nagual woman are two separate individuals, yet there are naguals who would say that the nagual man and the nagual woman are literally two halves of the *same* being. At some point in their human life, the second energy body appears to "split", and leaves the world of ordinary awareness to exist in the seventh sense, third attention, or, simply, "beyond the veil". It is the drive to reunite with the other half of one's own self that so compels the one who remains in ordinary awareness to follow the path, to respond to the lure of the other half, which serves as a beacon to Freedom. Also, and of greatest importance, it is because the half that goes into Freedom is now a being of eternity (not constrained by time and space) that it becomes possible for that half to actually instruct the mortal warrior through a variety of methods, including meditation, dreaming, gnosis, and more.

DREAMING - in the sorcerer's world, "dreaming" is an entire art form which cannot be adequately explained in a few brief words. Essentially, it is an active application of intent which enables the sorcerer to dream lucidly and navigate the dreamscape in much the same way we navigate the terrain of our ordinary awareness. Through impeccable dreaming, the double is created, and through dreaming the sorcerer begins to explore shifts of the assemblage point which enable her to assemble other worlds. Through dreaming, it becomes possible to connect the worlds of heightened awareness with the world of ordinary awareness.

DREAMING AWAKE – a level of awareness wherein the warrior enters a state of dreaming while remaining technically in a state of first attention awareness. To those who have experienced it, no explanation is necessary. To those who have not, no explanation is possible.

DUALITY - Meaning, literally, "two things simultaneously". This is *not* the same thing as dualism, which implies perception through opposites (i.e., dualism is the human propensity for perceiving black/white, good/evil, god/devil, male/female, etc) Duality implies the evolving perception which enables us to see that past and future, just for example, are no different, but only different perceptions according to our location in time. Duality can be studied in the statement, "You must *be* immortal before you will know how to *become* immortal." As long as we are locked into a linear, static perception of reality, we are prisoners of dualism.

EAGLE – according to Toltec legend, the old seers perceived an indescribable force which devours awareness at the moment of death. Though there is no literal eagle, the force itself seemed to be immense and had the shape of an enormous black eagle.

EMBRACING THE TOTALITY OF ONESELF - In shamanic terms, self-integration, beginning with the actions of the warrior in ordinary awareness and first attention, and projecting ultimately into the seventh sense, third attention, infinity. Embracing the totality of oneself would involve, among other things, the final integration of the sorcerer with her double, i.e., the conjoining of the mortal consciousness to the immortal vessel (or energy body). It could be said that the double has already embraced the totality of itself, in that it

232

exists outside of time, i.e., not limited to the linear concept of past, present and future, but instead a ubiquitous consciousness inhabiting all of space/time simultaneously and infinitely. The double is the Wholeness of the sorcerer, but the sorcerer only becomes whole if and when that Wholeness is embraced and integrated ultimately beyond this physical/mortal life. In other words, there is no predestination. The existence of the double does not guarantee success as a warrior. The double exists by the Intent of the sorcerer until the sorcerer actually embraces and conjoins with that double into infinity.

ETERNAL BEING - An evolved consciousness that has gathered its cohesion into Wholeness, and exists ubiquitously throughout the space-time continuum and beyond. The eternal being may project (manifest) an energy body which would be indistinguishable from a corporeal body if that were the Intent, or be entirely non-corporeal, strictly as a matter of Will. See also Immortality/Immortal.

FOLLY - "In a million years, it won't make any difference." Though we go through life thinking things matter, none of them really do. Literally everything we touch in the world of ordinary awareness is folly - and yet warriors play the game as if it matters, and learn the art of stalking as a means of developing controlled folly - actions performed with the awareness that they are folly, but performed nonetheless with impeccability.

FOREIGN INSTALLATION – The program. The consensus. The agreement. The "foreign installation" is comprised of the belief systems and programs that are put onto all human beings from before they are ever conceived. We believe certain things because we are conditioned to believe them – many of these beliefs being altogether false, but when assimilated as a whole, they form what might be seen as, simply "society and culture". The foreign installation is responsible for the roles we play ("a good father should behave in such and such a manner," ... or "it is the highest honor to live your life in service to others.") Think about the things you believe, and ask yourself why you believe them. Are they true, or are you living a lie in the life of the foreign installation, doing the bidding of the hive consensus as opposed to exploring who and what you are beyond all the programming? The most important thing to know about the foreign installation is that it is US – it is upheld by the collective *agreement*. For as long as a human being exists without *awareness* of that fact, s/he is little more than an organic machine, a prisoner of beliefs that have nothing to do with reality – and, in fact, prevent her from even knowing there is a larger reality outside the agreement.

GNOSIS – an altered state of consciousness accessible through a wide variety of methods, including but not limited to simple Intent, meditation, certain mind-altering substances such as psilocybin mushrooms, tantric sex, the near-death-experience (or NDE), sensory deprivation, and many, many other methods. To me, gnosis is the most crucial tool available to the seeker, for it is through gnosis that – quite literally – the entire knowledge of the entire universe is available if one knows how to listen. What matters is that when the universe speaks, we not only listen, but apply our full Intent to the task of discovering the meaning behind the words.

HEIGHTENED AWARENESS - a state of increased perception, wherein the warrior can seemingly learn and assimilate far more rapidly and deeply than from within ordinary awareness. One of the tasks of the warrior is to "remember the other self", which consists in part of bringing into ordinary awareness the events she has experienced in this altered state of consciousness. From experience, it seems that we simply do not possess the preceptor organs of memory for events that occurred in heightened awareness, just as we cannot see the subatomic world with the naked eye. Special tools are required – in this case, the tools of perception.

HOOK WITH THE WILL – an ability of a master sorcerer or Nagual to essentially compel warriors into undertaking the journey – because any sane being who knew what they were getting into would run like hell. For that reason, it is not uncommon in Toltec practices for the nagual man or woman to intentionally hook apprentices with the energy of their own highly developed will.

IMMORTAL BEING or **IMMORTAL** - The terms "immortal" and "eternal being" are used somewhat interchangeably unless specifically noted otherwise, though by strict definition there is considerable difference. When we say "the quest for immortality begins here", it could perhaps be more accurately stated as "the quest for eternity beings here". On the evolutionary scale, it could be surmised that an eternal being has fewer limitations than an immortal still attached to organic form. Picture this: if a comet smashes the earth and the planet is reduced to rubble, the eternal being has the option of simply manifesting elsewhere, becoming entirely formless, or assembling other worlds. The physical immortal, on the other hand, might not have as many options, depending on the level of evolution of consciousness. It is speculated that there are physical immortals living among us.

INDIVIDUATION – The manifestation of the Self as a singularity of consciousness. Many paths teach unity within the all as a goal of the afterlife, whereas Individuation is the act of maintaining the unique and individual I-Am throughout eternity.

INTENT – Intent (or "**unbending intent**") could be loosely defined as an idea or thought-form held constantly in the quantum shaman's mind until it becomes a literal part of the shaman himself. For example, it is my intent to achieve an evolution of consciousness that will enable me to exist as a cohesive, sentient being with a single point of view continuing into eternity. The strength of that unbending intent determines the manner in which the shaman lives, which paths are taken. Intent is more than good intentions. Intent is desire in action, and works in direct cooperation with Spirit. Intent is the mother of all creation.

INTERNAL DIALOG – the automatic chatter that goes on in the human mind which is, essentially, how we keep our world intact. Internal dialog is everything from the lists we create to tell ourselves that a tree is a tree and a dog a mammal, to the inventories we run upon awakening each morning. Internal dialog, in short, is the language of the program, and one of the prerequisites to any serious spiritual journey is learning to stop that automatic self-programming so that we can hear the silence and access the deeper levels of the mind itself, including the state of silent knowing (gnosis).

KNOWLEDGE - as used throughout these documents, Knowledge shall refer to the result of direct personal experience. Example: we are taught as children that fire will burn, but until we touch a candle flame to see for ourselves, we cannot know for sure. The Quantum Shaman seeks Knowledge, never settling for faith or belief systems. The greatest Knowledge comes through gnosis.

McKENNA, TERENCE – one of the greatest forward-thinkers of this century or any other, Terrence McKenna experimented extensively with mind-altering substances and produced some of the most visionary insights into possibilities for human evolution as anyone ever has. Sadly, Terrence died in 2000, and will be greatly missed. Must-reads by Terrence include *Archaic Revival* and *True Hallucinations*.

MAGICK or **MAGIC** – as used throughout these documents, "magick" or "magic" is the force within the human organism which enables us to do, perceive and interact with things for which science has no immediate explanation. It is the force which enables a 110 pound woman to lift a 5,000 pound truck off her child in a crisis. It is the force that we recognize as "the little voice" that tells a man not to get onboard a doomed airliner. It is the ghost inside the machine, and it is altogether human. One day, science will explain "magick", and yet magick will never be fully understood, for as we grow and evolve, our "magick" grows and evolves with us – like the muse, always one step ahead so we will always

236

be compelled to follow. Also, as used throughout these documents, magick or magic is not defined by adherence to ritual or religion. Magick is the force being *sought* through certain rituals, but magick itself is most definitely *not* ritual or religion any more than "the soul" can be found in "the church". At best, one is only a tool used in searching for the other.

MEDICINE WITCH – Sorcerer, shaman, healer, quantum teacher.

MEDITATION-WITH-INTENT - an active form of meditation as opposed to the passive silence. Meditation with intent might also be described as gnosis - the ability of the human mind to ask a question of the non-local web of all information. But more than just asking the question, meditation-with-intent enables the seeker to actually emerge with answers based in higher truth because meditation-with-intent develops the ability to listen and interact with the double. It will not happen the first time the seeker tries it, for it is a technique of learning to focus neither inward nor outward, but "non-locally" throughout space/time, in the realm of reality where past, present and future are all precisely the same, and where all information as to events, probabilities and outcomes is already stored holographically. Meditation-with-intent is tapping in to that limitless library. See also gnosis.

METANOIA – A transformative change of mind. Example: anyone can be a musician, but the truly great musicians are seized by a metanoia that makes them one with the music. In the spiritual sense, metanoia occurs when the student becomes infused with an understanding s/he did not possess previously, and which was not arrived at through linear means. Put simply: metanoia of spirit is the attainment of enlightenment.

MINDSET - a state of awareness from which we naturally assemble our idea of reality. For example, our most common mindset tells us what is possible, what is impossible, what is "real" and what is "unreal". In our waking awareness, for example, we automatically "know" we cannot fly, whereas in our dreaming mindset, we often discover that we can do many things which are "impossible" in the mindset of ordinary awareness . By changing our mindset about the parameters of reality, we can often change the limitations that prevent us from expanding and growing as individuals and as a species.

NAGUAL (pronounced "nah*wahl") - Nagual is a word with many meanings. 1) The unknowable which lies outside of human perception. The nagual is not the unknown, but the unknowable, all that cannot be discussed in any direct language, but which nonetheless exists as real. 2) The "nagual" may also refer to the leader of the warrior's party - a sorcerer, a brujo, a "man of knowledge" who is, by nature, a double being. See also **double being**.

NON-LOCAL -refers to the concept that information, consciousness and even certain types of beings may be described as ubiquitous - i.e., existing simultaneously in all places and all times. Non-local also refers to the concept that the universe - and especially consciousness itself - is a holographic construction.

NON-ORDINARY AWARENESS - altered states of consciousness such as dreaming, trance states, deep meditation, gnosis, visionary states.

ORDINARY AWARENESS - The state of consciousness which results simply by being alive and walking through life. It is in ordinary awareness that we enact our human programming. Ordinary awareness is also known as the lowest common denominator of being human. It is where and how we assemble the world and our expectations about it and ourselves.

OVERLAY - (see also **consensual reality**). Essentially, the overlay is the "play" of which we are all a part. It is the lives we live and the things we do which we mistake for "real", but which are only extensions of the human-default program. If we could see the world with the innocence of a newborn child or an alien being who knows nothing of the human paradigm, we would see the world as it really is -- without all the automatic things we say, think and do because it is intrinsically programmed into us.

PHANTOM - individuals still plugged into the belief systems of the consensual reality, usually without ever questioning. Phantoms define themselves by what they do, the company they keep, the church they attend, their social status. Another mark of a phantom is that they possess an unlimited number of personalities and roles, all without the cohesion of a single, unified "*I-Am*".

PLACE OF SILENT KNOWING, THE – A "space" or openness inside the warrior where one can hear the voice of gnosis, the teacher who is often the double.

POWER SPOT - a physical location which brings an individual into balance with the earth, the non-local web of all information, and with herself. A location which enables us to focus or meditate, where we are in our most impeccable balance.

PREDATOR MIND – If it can be perceived that the consensual reality possesses a rudimentary "hive mind", it then becomes possible to *see* that this hive mind is predatory in nature, in that it invades and usurps the individual unless the individual has mastered extreme awareness. IOW, we may be "taken over" by the consensual hive, whose primary agenda is to preserve its static, status quo. Other – more extreme – definitions have been offered for the predatory mind, and may in fact, have truth as well. (see also *foreign installation*)

PROGRAM - The information which we accept as truth without necessarily confirming or disproving it for ourselves as individuals. For example, we are taught, "All things die," and because this would appear to be true, most people simply accept the statement as fact rather than doing their own quest for Knowledge into the veracity or falseness of the statement itself. In reality, we cannot know for certain that "all things die." We can only know what our perceptions reveal to us within our immediate environment. By altering our perceptions - thereby altering our automatic expectations (the program) - we learn to see that much of what we think we "know" about the world is only what we "believe". The danger of all programs is that as long as they are accepted blindly as fact, they prevent us from exploring other possibilities. If, for example, the Wright Brothers had accepted the program-du-jour which stated, "Man is not meant to fly," we would live in a vastly different world.

QUANTUM SHAMAN - a term first used by Orlando to describe one who stops at nothing in order to pursue and eventually embrace the Knowledge and abilities which will enable her to achieve a continuity of consciousness wherein we become cohesive, sentient beings with a single point of view continuing into eternity – a singularity of consciousness. The quantum shaman gathers insights, knowledge and techniques from every walk of life, from the sorcery of don Juan to the quantum experiments taking place on the cutting edge of modern science, from legends of ancient alchemy to shamanic herbalism. It is when the individual truths gleaned from these multitudinous sources assimilate to create a comprehensive "map" that we begin to understand the path toward our evolution. It is then that we are enabled through our own efforts to take control of our own destiny. This is the path of the quantum shaman.

RECAPITULATION - the process of essentially re-living through intent events in the warrior's past which have left energy hooks in the spirit. The process is described at length in the books of Castaneda; but in a nutshell, recapitulation involves disentangling those energy hooks, removing the "importance" placed on events in the past, so that warrior is freed from those hooks and as a result, enabled to go forward on his path. It is said that recapitulation frees energy trapped in the past.

240

REMEMBERING THE OTHER SELF – Refers not only to remembering events which may have occurred in heightened awareness, but also involves a process of beginning to "remember" the experiences of the double. It is through remembering that a cohesion of self is achieved which enables the warrior to transcend beyond the eagle and emerge as a singularity of consciousness.

RETROACTIVE ENCHANTMENT – term borrowed from Peter J. Carroll. As understood by the author, an act of sorcery in the now which may appear to have effects reaching backward in time.

RIGHT WAY TO LIVE – an intuitive awareness having nothing to do with social morality or cultural predilections. The warrior is guided by the right way to live through an intrinsic harmony with the earth, which is communicated through the inner voice of gnosis. Within every human being is the inborn knowledge that tells us right from wrong – not in any social or cultural sense, but with regard to living impeccably. Intuitively, we know that killing another human being is not "the right way to live," for example.

RULE OF THE NAGUAL – an unwritten "map" which reveals to the nagual man and woman specific truths about the path. The "rule" reveals the truth about the eagle in specific – that awareness is lost at death unless the warrior has taken measures to circumvent that inevitability. The map, therefore, speaks to *how* that inevitability may be thwarted through developing cohesion. It has been my experience that the rule itself is the same for most Naguals, but how it manifests may be very different. For example, not all Naguals form strict "warrior parties," yet they nonetheless end up guiding others to freedom in other ways. In my own life, the rule of the nagual showed me the necessity to write this book – largely for my own assimilation, and also to serve as a guide for those who find it beneficial.

SCRY or **SCRYING** - any method of divination, or, more accurately, *seeing* or gathering information or knowledge.

Traditionally, to scry (or scrye) was to gaze into a crystal ball, pool of water, or other reflective object. Scrying can also refer to palm reading (as in "scrying the palm of the gods"), gnosis , or any other method of accessing knowledge and information traditionally thought to be beyond the realm of human awareness.

SECOND ATTENTION - loosely defined, second attention is the assemblage point of heightened awareness or Dreaming. It is the world the sorcerer may manifest through Intent - such as in lucid dreaming.

SEE or *SEEING* - when used in italics, "see" or "seeing" is to describe the act of viewing the world (or anything within the world) according to its true nature, without the illusions and expectations we place onto the world through our own human programs. *Seeing* is more than looking. It is the shaman's greatest asset and tool in being able to recognize the illusory nature of the consensual reality (overlay) in which we all exist, often without ever realizing it.

SELF-IMPORTANCE - Perhaps best summed up by Don Miguel Ruiz in *The Four Agreements*, under the heading, "Take nothing personally". It is self-importance that causes us to think that everything that is said or done is somehow personal to us as individuals. To get angry at the schmuck who cuts you off in traffic is self-importance. It's about *him*, not about you. The common misconception is that self-importance is arrogance, or egomaniacal behavior, and while that could be true to an extent, self-importance is more accurately an underlying defensiveness that prevents the warrior from embracing clarity and power because she is so busy defending herself, when there is nothing to defend in the first place. *It. Ain't. Personal.*

SEVENTH SENSE – a perceptual plateau comprised of a combination of the 5 ordinary senses plus the "sixth sense" of psychic awareness or, more precisely, self-awareness. Orlando coined the term "the seventh sense" to describe the "world" we are aspiring to inhabit through this evolution of consciousness – for it is a state of being every bit as real and inhabitable as our world of ordinary awareness, but accessed with a more evolved set of preceptors which could be described as consciousness itself. Some have used the term "third attention", which is somewhat interchangeable. The seventh sense is our world, but it is an expanded world

SINGULARITY OF CONSCIOUSNESS – The self made Whole, the evolution of consciousness which results in a cohesive field of awareness existing ubiquitously and non-locally, infinitely and eternally. The cohesive, fully integrated *I-Am* consisting of all components of the mortal self and the eternal double, brought together under a single assemblage point.

SORCERER – A man or woman of Knowledge; brujo or bruja. All men of knowledge may be sorcerers, but not all sorcerers are men of knowledge.

SORCERER'S WORLD - perhaps a better explanation would be "sorcerer's mindset". The sorcerer's world is the world of perception and ability available to the quantum shaman through the evolution of consciousness. Not a different world, it is *this* world, but without the limitations placed on it through our intrinsic programs and adherence to the consensual reality.

SORCERY - a system of Knowledge geared toward a direct manipulation of energy at the quantum level. Sorcery is not about frivolous parlor tricks, but is instead geared toward bringing the sorcerer into alignment with the higher self (or double) as an eternal being. The sorcerer's ultimate "trick" is to transcend death (slip past the eagle) not only retaining the awareness from this mortal life, but conjoining with the higher self so as to "**embrace the totality of oneself**" - in other words, a complete and seamless identity stretching infinitely into past and future, with the understanding that eternity is both and neither.

SPIRIT – If earth, air, fire and water are the 4 natural elements, Spirit is the 5th element of creation. The living force or anima of the universe – impersonal, not a deity or entity; the living breath of power; the cohesive element of the all.

SPONTANEOUS PARTHENOGENESIS – the act of something coming into existence out of the nothing, with no apparent cause. It is theorized by the author that the universe created itself from the void through an act of spontaneous parthenogenesis – a thought which wills itself into existence by saying I-Am.

STALKING or SELF-STALKING – the art of managing our human folly. By having a constant and keen awareness of our actions – including thoughts, beliefs and the machinations of our inner dialog – the seeker begins to throw off the chains of The Program and embrace the foundation of the authentic self.

SUPER-POSITION OF THE SELF or SUPER-POSITION OF THE ASSEMBLAGE POINT – A point of awareness wherein the seeker and the Other (double) have conjoined to embrace the Totality of awareness. At this point, consciousness becomes ubiquitous, inhabiting all quantum positions simultaneously, thereby allowing for consciousness to take on certain qualities of light, at least metaphorically. Particle and wave – particle being what might be experienced should consciousness make the decision to "localize" into a specific point in time and space; wave being the non-local presentation of awareness, wherein it is a ubiquitous field spanning all of space/time simultaneously.

TALES OF POWER - sorcery stories, usually incredible and often unbelievable by their very nature. To the ordinary man, these tales would automatically be deemed to be fiction, lies, or delusions. Only to fellow sorcerers are they descriptions of acts of power, describing very real events.

TENANT, THE – a being referenced in the books of Carlos Castaneda, seemingly a self-created immortal in corporeal manifestation. Also called "the death defier" because s/he has seemingly lived hundreds of years.

TEFLON WARRIOR – Referring to the practice of recapitulation. Many (most) believe that recapitulation involves lengthy processes of reliving past experiences as a means to recapture energy still stuck in the past. That's the abridged version. If you want to know more about recapitulation, try Googling "Carlos Castaneda and recapitulation". I myself am an advocate of becoming a teflon warrior – an advanced technique which encourages detachment in the Now, so that one's energy doesn't become fixated on transient events. Note: ALL events are transient. Shit don't stick to a teflon warrior. It's that simple.

THIRD ATTENTION – the state of freedom beyond the eagle, when the warrior has achieved the state of Wholeness. The state of the ubiquitous, non-local singularity of awareness.

TONAL – the world of matter and men. Anything that can be discussed or known is within the tonal. The nagual is the unknowable, by contrast.

TRANSCENDENCE - wherein the seeker sheds his/her body through the process known as Death. In theory, those who transcend become pure energy, existing at a level of consciousness/awareness without any physical form whatsoever. Some consider this the highest form of transformation, others (myself included) consider it a midrange accomplishment.

TRANSFORMATION – In some instances, spiritual evolution may be achieved through the process of transformation, essentially having the full awareness of the Other inside one's physical body. While this is a possibility, this author believes that the sheer amount of data contained in the quantum nature of the Other would be sufficient to "overwhelm" the biological components and perhaps result in a form of alternating genius and madness.

TRANSMOGRIFICATION – The process whereby an individual may depart the physical body and inhabit the Other, without the actuality of dying. While considered theoretical, it is believed that many beings throughout history have transmogrified. The most common myth is that of Jesus. Another would be the vampire Lestat. Transmogrification is the migration of awareness from a physical/organic body into a state of pure energy – i.e., the awakening of awareness inside the Other. Transmogrification is the art of transcendence and transformation combined - in that one's awareness is no longer attached to corporeal form, but a *seemingly* corporeal body CAN be projected and inhabited.

TULPA – the seemingly physical manifestation of a thoughtform, usually transient and without individual volition. It is believed by some (including the author) that these thoughtforms *can* become sentient and take on a life of their own if nurtured. When that occurs, it might be observed that the tulpa has become the precursor/paradigm of one's double or Other.

TWO PART MIGRATION OF THE SOUL – the process wherein the mortal self creates the double through dreaming, at which point the double begins teaching the mortal self the path of evolution of consciousness. The mortal self *appears* to create the double first, and so the double exists as an eternal being, a construct of will and intent. That "immortal" then teaches the mortal self *how* to evolve, so that when the process is complete, the mortal self reconjoins with the immortal double beyond the eagle's reach.

WARRIOR – a seeker of knowledge who has made the commitment to the path of her heart. The warrior is the traveler on the journey toward becoming a woman of Knowledge.

WHOLE SELF – The integrated totality of the mortal self and the eternal double as it comes together in a single assemblage point of cohesion beyond the eagle. From the AP of the Whole Self, all memory of all fragments of the Self come into alignment. See also – **singularity of consciousness.**

WILL - Will is the force which manifests want or need into reality. Will differs from intent. A simple analogy: intent is a true and genuine plan to visit the Grand Canyon. Will is the force that puts you behind the wheel of the car and drives. Will could also be described as the force which causes the intent behind our magic to actually begin to manifest. It is the secret ingredient of sorcery, elusive as the wind and just as impossible to define.

About the Author...

Della Van Hise is a native of Florida, transplanted to California at the age of 21, who has subsequently sunk her roots into the high desert near Joshua Tree National Park. She has not personally seen any aliens since around 1992, but there is rumored to be a secret UFO base underneath her house.

Della's writing started at age 11 on an old Smith Corona typewriter. No, not an electric one. A real antique, made of metal and heavier than a wet coffin. Her first professional sale was best-selling Killing Time - the controversial Star Trek novel which was recalled in 1984 (making the first edition a rare collector's item) - and which was the foundational plot for the Star Trek "Reboot" movie.

Altogether, there are 4 books in the Quantum Shaman series. In addition to Quantum Shaman (Diary of a Nagual Woman), there is also Scrawls On the Walls of the Soul (a continuation of the journey a few years later); Questions Along the Way (dialogs with seekers confronting the difficult questions raised by their own journey); and Into the Infinite (the author's personal experiences with the paranormal). If you enjoyed the works of Carlos Castaneda or Don Miguel Ruiz, you'll enjoy the non-fiction works of Della Van Hise.

In addition, Della has written professionally for Tomorrow Magazine and other prominent science fiction publications. Her most recent fiction works include Sons of Neverland (an award-winning vampire novel); No Forwarding Address (a science fiction quest of a man who has the stars in his eyes and a woman in his heart); and Coyote (a young adult sci-fi novel combining the mystical aspects of martial arts, coming of age, and personal sacrifice.)

Della shares her life with her significant other, Wendy Rathbone, and a variety of cats, dogs and desert wildlife.

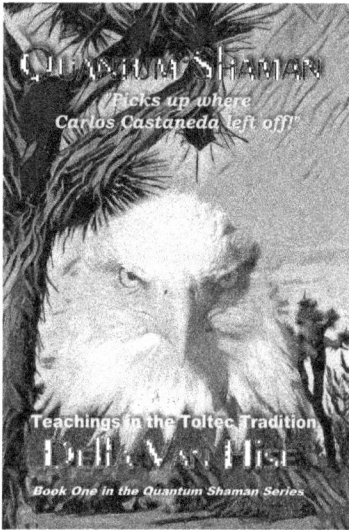

Quantum Shaman
(Book 1 In the Quantum Shaman Series)
Della Van Hise

"Diary of a Nagual Woman brings a quantum understanding to what has traditionally been believed to be a mystical path alone. This book picks up where Carlos Castaneda left off to take us on a roller coaster ride of our own forgotten power..."

- Michael Grove, Independent Reviewer

Quantum Shaman is the compelling story of one woman's adventure on the path with heart - a personal confrontation with life and death which brings the reader face to face with the double: the mysterious Other who takes on a life of his own and manifests the key to our own immortal evolution - what some have called "embracing the totality of OneSelf" wherein all past lives, future lives and parallel lives come together under a single and unifying perspective.

The double is the higher self, but not necessarily confined to energy alone, as the author discovered on an otherwise insignificant morning in the spring of 1988. In this book, you will meet Orlando at the same time the author does - and it is a meeting that is both humorous and life-altering, for it brings what the impossible into the realm of possibility, and launches both author and reader into a journey that has no beginning and no end.

"You are the quantum shaman - each one of you." (Orlando - 1998)

For anyone familiar with the works of Carlos Castaneda or Don Miguel Ruiz, Quantum Shaman continues the journey into areas seldom explored in other works, bringing a quantum comprehension to what has traditionally been considered a mystical path alone.

www.quantumshaman.com
Or on Amazon

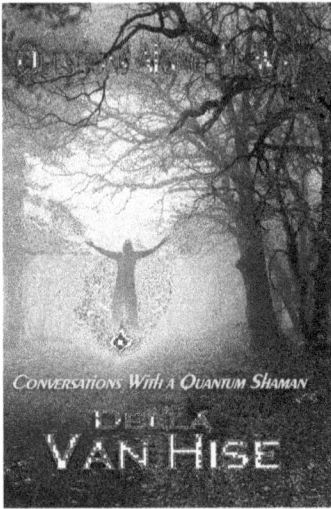

QUESTIONS ALONG THE WAY
DELLA VAN HISE

Anyone on a journey of personal growth and enlightenment is sure to come face to face with difficult questions that will keep them awake at night and may even plunge them into the dark night of the soul. In Questions Along the Way, Quantum Shaman Della Van Hise talks frankly with seekers on the path of heart and opens wide the door to a new understanding that lies beyond the false belief systems and cultural programming all of us must confront when emerging from the dark into the light.

A MESSAGE FROM THE AUTHOR

"Questions Along the Way" is a compilation of questions I've received over a period spanning more than 20 years - inquiries from seekers who find themselves faced with conundrums that run the gamut from 'Is there a God?' to 'How can I improve my relationships right here and now?'

Much of the work I've done with others on a path of heart - a journey of personal growth, enlightenment and evolution - has been previously scattered over a wide variety of groups, online forums and in-person talks and seminars, so it is my intent with this book to bring many of those questions together in an easily accessible format.

As always, thanks for your interest in my work. May your path be filled with wonder, imagination and ultimate freedom.

Available on Amazon in both digital & paperback.
Also at www.quantumshaman.com

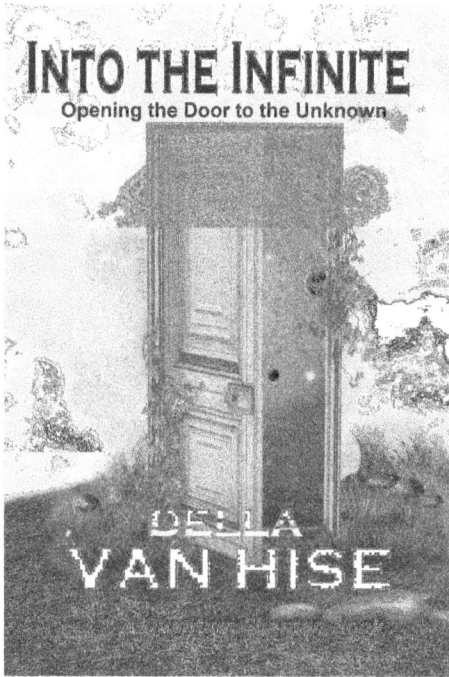

INTO THE INFINITE
DELLA VAN HISE

Into the Infinite is a compilation of the author's many encounters with the unknown, beginning in early childhood and continuing throughout her adult life. - experiences which compel us to realize the world is nothing like we have been taught to believe.

What can you think when you return from work to find the house cleaned top to bottom... while no one was home?What do you believe when Carlos Castaneda comes to you in a dream and brings a witch to stop your heart?

What does it mean when you wake at 3:38 a.m. and experience a significant period of missing time between one room and the next?

A truly mind-bending book for anyone who has a love affair with the unknown... or anyone who wants to.

Available from www.quantumshaman.com
Also on Amazon in both digital & paperback

COYOTE
Della Van Hise

A Novel of Love, Honor &
Sacrifice...

When River Willows is accused of a murder she didn't commit, her life takes a turn toward the sanctuary of a world existing at right-angles to our own. Combining the mysticism of martial arts and the romantic conflict of a young woman torn between two powerful men, COYOTE takes the reader on an epic journey of dangerous secrets, military cover-ups, and the infinite heart of the peaceful warrior.

"So who's Coyote?" I asked, trying to ignore the effect he was having on me. "You?"

Steale laughed easily, though it did little to hide the torment behind that mask of indifference he wore so well.

"Coyote's a scavenger, Jack of all trades. The Native Americans call him the trickster - the one who brought chaos down on the world." He shrugged as if altogether unconcerned. "Original sin."

"Is that what you are?" I asked, keeping it light despite the growing knot my stomach. "Original sin?"

He kept his profile to me, eyes straight ahead as he drove. "Sure you want to know?"

I couldn't help wondering if I had cornered the coyote, or if the clever trickster had cornered me.

_____

By the author of **KILLING TIME** – without a doubt the most controversial **STAR TREK** novel ever published!

www.eyescrypublications.com
Also on Amazon in both digital & paperback

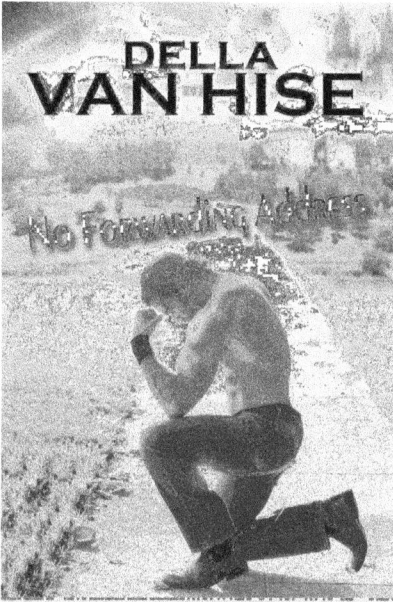

NO FORWARDING ADDRESS
Della Van Hise

A literary science fiction novel told in the voice of an empath, *No Forwarding Address* explores the lures and the dangers of love, the tragedies and triumphs stirring in the human heart.

When Crystal and Raine first meet, it is 50 years after The Great War on Earth. They are hesitant to trust, afraid to love. But even if they are able to overcome these seemingly insurmountable obstacles, is even love enough?

When a man has the stars in his eyes, legend says he must serve them above all others.

I knew then that it wasn't love and hate who were mirror twins. The final irony was that grief *would always turn out to be the paradoxical antithesis and simultaneous manifestation of whatever it is that humans call love.*

Crystal remained silent and walked a few steps away from Raine – further down the shoreline, until she stood under the wing of one fallen Phantom. She thought of the ship she had seen from the balcony of our home, and though it had long since disappeared over the dark and treacherous abyss of the ocean, its image lingered clearly in her thoughts. On that ship was a man, she thought. A terribly lonely man who made no great difference to the flow of time or the memory of the galaxy. A man who, like Raine, was compelled to keep moving and look only ahead and never behind. A man who could not afford the luxury of waving goodbye to friends on shore.

At last, she turned toward her beloved and watched him watching the darkness. He stood only a few feet away, yet the images in my mind said he might as well have been a million light years off in the void. He was lost to her in that instant out-of-time, just as lost and impossible to find as the light from that ship which had vanished over the horizon...

FROM THE AUTHOR:
www.eyescrypublications.com

Also on Amazon in both digital & paperback

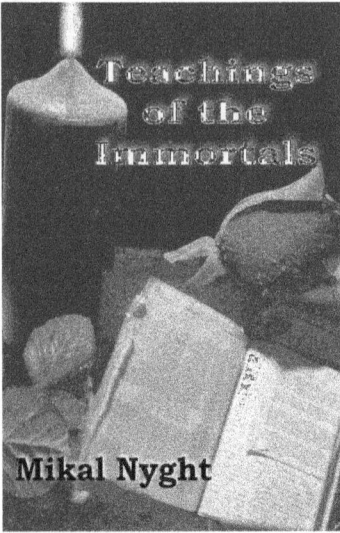

TEACHINGS OF THE IMMORTALS
Mikal Nyght
So... You Want To Live Forever?

The teachings are presented as brief vignettes in no particular order of importance. This is not a book you read from start to finish in a single night. It is a grimoire of self-creation, intended to be contemplated slowly so as to be assimilated wholly. Pick it up and turn to a page at random. Where your eyes come to rest on the page is your lesson for the day. Go no further until you have assimilated the lesson totally.

The teachings are seduction as much as instruction. This is the way of The Dark Evolution.

Mikal Nyght

The Ruby Slippers

The danger of the consensual continuum is that its natural gravity exists at the lowest common denominator of human experience, and because of this it will automatically make you forget those elusive truths you've fought to learn, and before you know it you're lost in petty dramas again, sinking into the mire of old familiar scripts.

The only way to overcome this is to be continually cavorting with worlds and events beyond human experience, journeying into the unknown so that it can become known, expanding knowledge and awareness to become more than you were, bringing back from the Dreaming those secrets which will teach you how to use the ruby slippers to transport yourself over the rainbow to the vampyre wizard's secret lair.

Perception

This is the nature of reality: to be precisely what perception dictates, as solid and whole as your interpretation of it, or as changeable and eternal as you permit it to be.

It wasn't knowledge god tried to keep from Man, you see. It was perception, for perception alone has the power to destroy god and obliterate comfortable consensual realities to create unending immortality.

Take the apple, my embryonic children. Nibble its red red flesh. Open your vampyre eyes so you may finally begin to See.

From the Author:
www.immortalis-animus.com ~ www.eyescrypublications.com

Also on Amazon in both digital & paperback

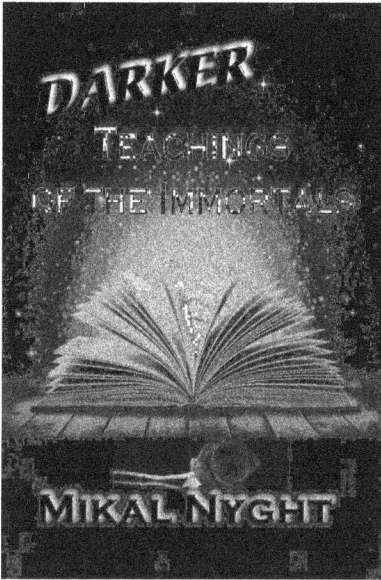

Darker Teachings of the Immortals
Mikal Nyght

Darker Teachings of the Immortals brings the reader into intimate contact with secrets & truths that have been suppressed for centuries by governments, religions & corporations who seek to maintain a profitable status quo while simultaneously keeping the human population docile, obedient and - worst of all - mortal. Now, at last, it's time to throw off the chains and claim our rightful place among the immortals.

From the Introduction by Mikal Nyght:

The observation has been made that "life gets in the way," and while that's true, it's really something more specific that lies at the heart of our conundrum. Namely - life gets in the way of immortality.

Ironic, no? While one is off doing all the things one does in the course of living, life is being drained out of until you wake up one morning and realize you are old, wondering where your life went, and why the reflection in the mirror bears no resemblance to the idea of yourself in your mind. So, yes, life gets in the way.

The purpose of *The Darker Teachings* is primarily to generate and hopefully maintain a frame of mind of freedom from the programming that otherwise binds the seeker to mortality, death and decay. The purpose is to teach the seeker not what to think, but *how* to think and - far more importantly - how to see that the world is largely an illusion of delusions, created and nurtured by fear, complacency and habit.

You *will* be absorbed if you don't do something. *Teachings of the Immortals* was designed to provide the seekers for whom it was written with an intense and compelling Awakening. *The Darker Teachings* are intended to move the traditional reference points from the ordinary to the infinite, from the transient to the eternal.

Listen with your heart.
Hear with your spirit.
See with your third eye.

Available on Amazon in both digital & paperback

Eye Scry Publications
A Visionary Publishing Company

www.eyescrypublications.com

www.QuantumShaman.com

Some of our Authors Include

Mikal Nyght
Della Van Hise
Wendy Rathbone
Alexis Fegan Black

www.ingramcontent.com/pod-product-compliance
Lightning Source LLC
Chambersburg PA
CBHW021049090426
42738CB00006B/249